Anthony Duncan is the author of *The Mind of Christ* and *The Whole Christ* as well as a number of other notable Christian titles. He is an Anglican canon of Scottish descent, now living in Northumberland.

The *Elements of* is a series designed to present high quality introductions to a broad range of essential subjects.

The books are commissioned specifically from experts in their fields. They provide readable and often unique views of the various topics covered, and are therefore of interest both to those who have some knowledge of the subject, as well as to those who are approaching it for the first time.

Many of these concise yet comprehensive books have practical suggestions and exercises which allow personal experience as well as theoretical understanding, and offer a valuable source of information on many important themes.

In the same series

> **the elements of**

celtic christianity

anthony duncan

ELEMENT

Shaftesbury, Dorset • Boston, Massachusetts • Melbourne, Victoria

© Element Books Limited 1992
Text © Anthony Duncan 1992

First published in Great Britain in 1992 by
Element Books Limited
Shaftesbury, Dorset SP7 8BP

Published in the USA in 1992 by
Element Books, Inc.
160 North Washington Street, Boston, MA 02114

Published in Australia in 1992 by
Element Books
and distributed by Penguin Australia Ltd
487 Maroondah Highway, Ringwood, Victoria 3134

Reprinted 1993
Reprinted 1994
Reprinted March and September 1995

Reissued 1997
Reprinted 1998

Cover Photograph: Combelin Stone, Nargam Abbey,
West Glamorgan
Courtesy of The National Museum of Wales
Cover design by Max Fairbrother
Typeset by Falcon Typographic Art, Fife, Scotland
Printed and bound in Great Britain by
Biddles Ltd, Guildford and King's Lynn

British Library Cataloguing in Publication
Data available

Library of Congress Cataloging in Publication Data
The elements of Celtic Christianity/Anthony Duncan
Includes bibliographical references and index.
1. Celtic Church. 2. Ireland–Religion.
1. Title. II. Title: Celtic Christianity. III. Series.
BR737.C4D86 1992
274.1'01–dc20 92–323111

ISBN 1–86204–138–5

CONTENTS

For Colmcille, Brother-in-Christ and
tribal kinsman

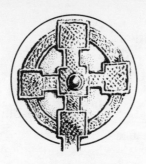

ACKNOWLEDGEMENTS

The quotations from Celtic sources, upon which this work substantially depends, derive largely from the work of Alexander Carmichael (b. 1832). During the course of a long life, Carmichael collected from the people of the Highlands and Islands of Scotland their traditions, their prayers and their poetry, all of which he eventually published in the six large volumes of his *Carmina Gadelica*.

Many others have published selections from this massive source and I have made use of this material as found in *The Celtic Vision*, edited by Esther De Waal, in *Poems of the Western Highlanders* by G.R.D. McLean, and in a selection from this latter made by Sally Magnusson under the title *Praying with Highland Christians*.

Another major source for quotations has been the collection of translations from Celtic literature compiled by Kenneth Hurlstone Jackson, under the title *A Celtic Miscellany*.

A Welsh Pilgrim's Manual, edited by Brendan O'Malley, contains, among other treasures, excellent translations of more modern Welsh material, and I have also quoted from Thomas Kinsella's translation of the *Tain Bo Cuailnge*. Other quotations, from Bede and others, are noted as they occur.

All the sources referred to above are readily

available to the reader, mostly in inexpensive paperback editions.

All sources which I found immediately useful are acknowledged under *Textual References* and *Additional Sources* at the end of the book, but inevitably most of my material comes from the reading and enthusiasms of a lifetime and can no longer be specifically identified.

I acknowledge with gratitude the prayers and the encouragements of many brethren of like heart and mind. And I am happy to 'declare an interest' in that my somewhat remote forefathers were none other than those Irish 'Scotti' who once established the kingdom of Dalriada on the west coast and among the Islands of Scotland.

I am grateful to the following individuals and publishers for permission to quote from their works.

K. H. Jackson, *A Celtic Miscellany*, Routledge.

J. Marsden, *The Illustrated Columcille* Macmillan London.

R. S. Thomas, 'The Moor', *Pieta*, Rupert Hart Davis, London, 1966.

T. Kinsella, 'He is coming, Adzed-Head', *New Oxford Book of Irish Verse*, Oxford University Press.

B. O'Malley (ed.), S. and C. Davies (trans.), *A Welsh Pilgrim's Manual*, Gomer Press, 1989.

'Jesu MacMary, Have mercy upon us', 'The Three who are over my head', *Praying with the Highland Christians*, Triangle Books/SPCK, © The Estate of G. R. D. Maclean, 1961, 1988.

A. Carmichael, *Carmina Gadelica*, Scottish Academic Press.

1 · THE RELEVANCE OF OUR CELTIC ROOTS

Greetings to you, new moon, darling of my love!
Greetings to you, new moon, darling of graces.

You journey on your course, you steer the flood-tides,
You light up your face for us, new moon of the seasons.

Traditional Gaelic[1]

The Kalahari bushmen have a phrase for it: with the unerring accuracy of the aboriginal they sum up the longing of late twentieth-century Western man. Approaching in some to the point of desperation, it is an increasingly felt longing: 'to walk again with the moon and the stars'.

Two closely connected tragedies confront us, both of them coming more and more insistently into conscious awareness. The first is the nightmarish rape of the earth itself; the second is the schizoid separation of organized religion from life, and its consequent retreat into what all too often seems to be a complete irrelevance.

Late twentieth-century Western man seems to have

1

fallen collectively into that state most feared of all by his African brother – he has 'lost his soul'. And even if he has not in fact quite lost it yet, then a great many individuals among the multitude are in extreme anxiety lest he shall, finally and irrevocably, do so.

'The Church doesn't seem to have anything to do with God!' So said more than one young adult to me towards the end of the 1960s. And the writer Laurens Van Der Post, writing a few years later, articulated what is still a very widespread experience:

> Ever since my childhood, the church into which I was born and all the other churches I encountered, far from promoting the natural interest I believe I have always had in religion, seemed to come down like an iron curtain between me and my own religious feelings . . . Wherever I went in the world I took great comfort in looking not only at Christian churches but also entering the temples of countries as far away as Ceylon, India and Japan . . . The trouble for me only began when I joined congregations in such places and was compelled to listen to priests and their utterances. Instantly I was dismayed, and whatever there had been of God in the church or temple fled.[2]

In Van Der Post's own Calvinistic background the utterances included much that was a stark denial of the goodness of Creation, an essential hatred of women and of 'the feminine' in general, and an outright identification of sex with sin. In various degrees of dilution, this selfsame, bleak and alienating doctrine can be met with throughout the whole spectrum of Western Christianity. Its contrast with the New Testament, both in letter and in spirit, is both stark and astonishing, and we shall return to this on a later page.

In about 1852, the President of the United States of America wrote to Chief Seattle to enquire about buying his tribal lands for the benefit of new settlers. In his reply the Chief asks questions both terrifying to the easy assumptions of Western civilization, and apocalyptic in their reproach to the religion of that most urgently church and chapel-going nation:

How can you buy or sell the sky? The land? . . . If we do not own the freshness of the air and the sparkles of the water, how can you buy them?

Every part of this earth is sacred to my people. Every shining pine needle, every sandy shore, every mist in the dark woods, every meadow, every humming insect. All are holy in the memory and instinct of my people. We know the sap which courses through the trees, as we know the blood which courses through our veins. We are part of the earth as the earth is part of us. The perfumed flowers are our sisters. The bear, the deer, the great eagle, these are our brothers. The rocky crests, the juices in the meadows, the body heat of a pony and man all belong to the same family.[3]

The Chief's letter continues at length, and with such a heartbroken compassion for the land which he knows he will be driven from, that it becomes almost unbearable to read. But it is not only the nineteenth-century American Indian who could find cause and compassion to write such a letter. Barely 250 years earlier, any Irish chieftain could have written it, under not dissimilar pressures, and in identical terms. And that Irish chieftain would have been a Christian of some thirteen hundred years' standing!

The Celts, like the American Indians, were tribal peoples to whom the concept of individual ownership – especially of land – was altogether alien. Far from them owning land, both peoples acknowledged the land as owning them!

Something has gone disastrously wrong – that much is clear beyond question. Where do we look to find the necessary inspiration to put it right?

However valuable the insights that come from the discovery of oriental and pagan traditions, they cannot of themselves provide the answer. We must search within our own Christian culture and its traditions, and it is my conviction that the Celtic Church and what we can describe as Celtic Christianity provide us with what, in all essentials, we are looking for.

It is first necessary, however, to become very clear about exactly what is meant by the terms 'the Celtic Church' and 'Celtic Christianity'.

THE CELTIC SPIRIT

Little antlered one, little belling one, melodious little bleater, sweet I think the lowing that you make in the glen.

Apple-tree, little apple-tree, violently everyone shakes you; rowan, little berried one, lovely is your bloom.

Bramble, little humped one, you do not grant fair terms; you do not cease tearing me till you are sated with blood!

Twelfth-century Irish[4]

At the beginning of the seventeenth century, no map had yet been drawn of the rocky coast of County Donegal, and surveyors and cartographers were therefore set to work. However, they went in fear of their lives for the native Irish were aghast at an impiety, a lack of respect for the land and its personality, its very elemental spirit, which could reduce it to marks on paper for the purpose of control.

Ireland provides the most recent, and perhaps the fullest, sources of information; but the Celtic Church, as encountered by much later Continental missions, was also found to be well established in Scotland (both Pictish and Irish-Scot), Wales, Cornwall and the west of England, Northumbria and the Isle of Man. It was the Church of the indigenous Celtic people of the British Isles and was the fulfilment of all that was good and true in the pre-Christian religions that had gone before.

In his monumental book on the Pictish Church and nation, Archibald Scott writes:

> The Picts, like all the Celts, were an emotional, imaginative, romantic and chivalrous people. They imparted into their practice of Christianity all the inherited vivacity of their race; and the points in the Christian faith to which they held most strongly were similar to the points to which they had attached themselves in the ancient pre-Christian religion of the Celts.[5]

And Frank Delaney, a more recent writer on the subject, writes:

> My Irish ancestors took to Christianity with ease, adroitness and piety. Given that the Celts were otherwise rebarbative in their own defence, spiritually and practically, it seemed to me at first glance surprising that they embraced the story of Christ with such facility – alacrity even.
>
> Not at all: religious belief supplied the oxygen in the Celtic aspiration to immortality, in their ambition to defeat death and the terror it brought. Christianity produced the hardest and most pragmatic development in the chain

of reconciliation, interpretation, morality and growth. Furthermore, it offered everything the Celts already had – and more.

The voyage from oaken grove to communion with Christ took several thousand years. Like a cabbalistic scroll it charts the Celtic, spiritual ascent through personal magic, tribal ritual, mythology, scripture. The earth itself was worshipped in dumb fright, and the spirit connected in awe with the inanimate – tree, river, rock. Ritualised recognition of the animate – beast and bird – was followed by a slow mythological shifting of shapes between animal and human.

Finally, just as Celtic civilization reached its apogee, the Celts encountered the Son of God. And – glory be! – he, it was found, was human like themselves and he surrounded himself with real people, the saints.

Here stood the ultimate compliment to Man for having made it safely out of the ooze. Now any mere human being, frail and flawed, could become immortal – and important for Heaven's sake! The terror of death was seen off by the promise of better things in a beautiful place, an alcove on the golden stairway.

And was all this new – this religion, this belief, this mythology, this faith? No: many of the impulses and the symbols of Celtic paganism received answer in Christianity.[6]

'The angels of Scripture captured the Celtic imagination.' writes Scott:

This was natural to a people whose ancient religion had taught them to look for spirits on mountain and moor, in tree and forest, in well and river, in lake and sea. The attachment of the name of Pictish saints to crags and trees, and wells, river-pools and lochans ... is not fully explained by the fact that they were associated with preachings and baptisms. The name of a saint often displaced the name of a supposed spirit that the Christian teachers desired to be forgotten.[7]

The love of his native land has always been a strong feature of the Celt. In the late fourth century, the Brito-Pictish tribe, the Votadini, were invited by the Romans south of Hadrian's Wall to undertake on their behalf the liberation of north Wales from the invading Irish. Their Chief, Cunedda, left one of his nine sons, Typiaun, in charge of the tribal lands in Scotland and marched into Wales with his other eight sons and their war-host.

From their new new home in Gwynedd, they recalled their old home and 'in their songs pictured the spirits of the departed as wandering in the woods of Celyddon (Caledonia). But, apart from scraps of literature, the Pictish place-names suffice to show how carefully the Pict marked and named the features of his country.'

The Celt is our own aborigine. He represents to us both the 'original inhabitant' of these islands and also the primitive origins of what is by now a thoroughly mixed-blooded race. He naturally relates his origins to myth rather than to history. And myth, rightly understood, is a poetic means of expressing a truth which cannot be adequately expressed in any other way. The Celt naturally expresses himself in poetry, while the Anglo-Saxon tends towards expression in essentially earthy flat prose. The two have vital need of each other, and it is as well that their blood is by now well and truly intermingled, for twentieth-century Western culture seems to have lost the vital ability to live by myth and symbol. It has lost contact with its own unconscious and has so far lost touch with its deeper self as to popularly identify the word 'myth' with 'lie'!

Yet even in the midst of this waterless desert, Delaney testifies:

> In my Irish Catholic boyhood we drank a curious soup of religion and mythology, rich and viscous but with a bitter-sweet taste, comforting yet warming. The ingredients – though never officially twinned – were the sober Christianity of Patrick and the wild paganism of the Celts. So close the relationship, so alive the pagan history of this Isle of Saints and Scholars, that if a bunch of time-travelling, horse-borne Celtic warriors had turned up at Mass on a Sunday morning my eyes would have been surprised – but not my imagination, nor my faith.[8]

This extract affirms that there is a wild and free spirit in the Celts. Perhaps some would smile indulgently at what they may be tempted to dismiss as Celtic ignorance and superstition. A second reaction could very well be the discovery of an unease within ourselves and a sense of something immeasurably precious having been lost. As the great prophet of our century, C.G. Jung, would be quick to point out, there is the threat of death in the initial dismissal, the death of our spirit . . .

In Biblical terms, the conflict between Celt and Anglo-Saxon, between Chief Seattle and the President of the United States of America, between the Irish heroic culture of the early seventeenth century and the urgently imported Scottish and northern English 'Planters', was in all essentials that between Cain and Abel – Cain, the agriculturalist, the expanding and self-styled 'owner' of land, in conflict with Abel the hunter–gatherer, the herdsman.

Our culture cannot put the clock back, nor can it un-invent its own instruments of destruction. But it can seek *now* to reconcile the Cain and Abel within itself, and try again to exercise the *Priesthood of Man* in the context of that integration. The Priesthood of Man is the responsibility laid upon the human race, in *Genesis* Chapter 1, to 'have dominion' over the earth as steward, manager, priest – to be responsible to God for other creatures.

The Celtic Christian tradition points the way, but we have to make it our own. This should not prove too difficult because, being deeply true to its New Testament source, it is perpetually contemporary. It is also – as any truly Christian tradition must be – uncompromisingly 'Green'. And what is it to be 'Green' if not to acknowledge a loving responsibility to Almighty God for Creation?

THE GOOD EARTH

> *I arise today*
> *Through the strength of heaven;*
> *Light of sun,*
> *Radiance of moon,*
> *Splendour of fire,*
> *Speed of lightning,*
> *Swiftness of wind,*
> *Depth of sea,*
> *Stability of earth,*
> *Firmness of rock.*
> Saint Patrick, 'The Cry of the Deer'[9]

So sang Saint Patrick in 'The Cry of the Deer', perhaps the greatest of all Celtic Christian hymns. And the Celtic vision is also admirably summed up in these words from the poet Gerard Manley Hopkins:

The world is charged with the grandeur of God.[10]

But not grandeur only – compassion, beauty, blessedness as well. There is no false division between the sacred and the secular – all is blessed. The whole of life, the whole of Creation is brim-full of the Divine Presence and there is nowhere where God is not.

The first obvious characteristic of Celtic Christianity is its affirmation of a Creation that is blessed. God saw all that he had made and *it was very good*. This is the uncompromising teaching of Holy Scripture from the very first page, and in that context the task of mankind in Creation is to 'increase and multiply, and have dominion'. In other words, mankind is created by God as steward, manager, priest and custodian of the created order of which he is an integral part. The labour given to mankind is the labour of love.

The Celtic heart and mind is consistant throughout the centuries. John Ceiriog Hughes, writing in the nineteenth century, might just as well have been writing in the ninth when he wrote:

Mountain stream, clear and limpid, wandering down towards the valley, whispering songs among the rushes – oh, that I were as the stream!

Mountain heather all in flower – longing fills me, at the sight, to stay upon the hills in the wind and the heather.

Small birds of the high mountains that soar up in the healthy wind, flitting from one peak to the other – oh, that I were as the bird!

Son of the mountain am I, far from home making my song; but my heart is in the mountain, with the heather and small birds.
                              J.C. Hughes (from the Welsh)[11]

The Celtic heart and mind, indeed the entire Celtic tradition, both Christian and pre-Christian, shares Chief Seattle's awareness that the land is sacred –

the earth is precious to God, and 'to harm the earth is to heap contempt on its creator'.

There is no false separation between 'religion' and 'life' in the Celtic Christian tradition; nor is there an inappropriate and unreal separation between Creation and Creator. To use the terms of theology, God is not only transcendant, He is immanent as well. To put it more simply, in the words of W.B. Yeats's 'Crazy Jane':

All things remain in God.[12]

Prayer is all-inclusive, as everything in Creation is the Celt's brother or sister:

O Son of God, do a miracle for me and change my heart; Thy having taken flesh to redeem me was more difficult than to transform my wickedness.

It is Thou who, to help me, didst go to be scourged . . .
Thou, dear child of Mary, art the refined molten metal of our forge.

It is Thou who makest the sun bright, together with the ice;
It is Thou who createdst the rivers and the salmon all along the river.

That the nut-tree should be flowering, O Christ, it is a rare craft;
Through thy skill too comes the kernel, Thou fair ear of our wheat.

Though the children of Eve ill deserve the bird-flocks and the salmon,
It was the Immortal One on the Cross who made both salmon and birds.

It is He who makes the flower of the sloes grow
through the surface of the blackthorn, and the
nut-flower on other trees;
Beside this, what miracle is greater?[13]

'O Son of God, do a miracle for me and change my heart' is the prayer, spoken or unspoken, of all Christian believers contemplating the rape of the good earth in the urgent service of the great god Mammon. (Mammon – the Syrian god of riches referred to by Jesus as representing the money-orientated life.) It is made all the more poignant by the realization of the profound and many-dimensioned failure of organized religion in this most fundamental of mankind's concerns.

Perhaps we should be neither surprised nor affronted by the terrible waking vision given to the twelve-year-old Carl Jung who saw the great cathedral of Basle, physically in his line of vision, shattered by a great fall of excrement from a golden throne in the sky!

There is, however, another change of heart to which the Celtic Christian tradition points: the rediscovery of the feminine principle, the acknowledgement by men of their own feminine nature, and the complementary release in women of their long suppressed and denied masculine nature and all the creativity which must accompany it.

WOMEN IN THE CELTIC TRADITION

There is mother's heart in the heart of God.

A Hebridean saying that says it all! There is to be found in the whole Celtic tradition a remarkable equilibrium as far as the masculine and the feminine are concerned. It is not a complete equilibrium but it is remarkably free from the man-dominated, woman-hating (which means woman-fearing) distortions which are to be found in many other cultures, and which survive, disfiguringly and unfaithfully, in many of the Churches of the Christian Church as a whole.

As Laurens Van Der Post testifies, in respect of his early enthusiasm for Freud which waned as the latter's metaphysics of sex became more and more prominent:

> Nothing should have made this aspect of Freud more plausible and its appeal greater than the puritanical Calvinist world into which I was born. There in a one-sided, man-dominated world sex was, at best, a necessary evil. The community's attitude was invested with *an abomination of it and women* [my italics] as great as that expressed by Calvin's fanatical disciple John Knox, whose Church really fathered the Dutch Reformed Church of my world and not that of the Holland of which it was ostensibly a branch.[14]

We should note in passing that this same John Knox was a Celt and founding father of the Church of Scotland. We shall have to return on a later page to this 'shadow side' of Celtic Christianity, but for the moment it is not our concern.

In the heroic Celtic culture, women did not 'have their place'. It was more nearly the case that men and women both had their place, and that of women does not seem to have been unduly man-dominated. Warrior queens were not uncommon, as the historical example of Boudicca testifies. And in the realm of myth, as well as in that shadowland where myth and history mingle, remarkably dominant and 'liberated' women abound.

King Ailil and Queen Medb of Connacht were of at least equal standing and, of the two, Medb is clearly the dominant. The great warrior hero Cuchulainn went from Ulster to Alba (Scotland) to learn the arts of war from a redoubtable woman called Scathach, who was currently at war with another warrior queen by the name of Aife.

It was into this context that the Christian Faith came, and almost at once remarkable women were to be found in positions of leadership within the Christian community. Bride of Kildare was one, Hilda of Whitby another, the latter being Anglo-Saxon by race but Celtic in religion.

Communities reflect their underlying myth and symbolism, and in this the Celts were fortunate. The mother-goddess was a powerful influence who kept the gods in equilibrium. And often identified with the mother-goddess was another goddess called Brigit or Bride – anciently the patron of poets, smiths and healers, she is the true mother of memory who fosters the creative and magical arts.

Brigit's feast was that of Oimelc (Imbolc) the 31st of January, the time of the failing of the winter's strength and the time of the birth of lambs. She then assumed the form of a beautiful young woman (as opposed to the hag of winter).

Brigit first became identified with Bride of Kildare (whose feast-day is the 1st of February) and then, to a greater or lesser degree, with the Blessed Virgin Mary in whom all the mother-goddess symbolisms find their fulfilment. Apocryphal stories see Brigit as a foster-mother of Christ, as one who helped Mary find him when lost in the temple, and so on. To add to the not-unhealthy confusion, Bride of Kildare is also sometimes known as 'Mary of the Gaels'!

In this woman-accepting, woman-honouring heroic culture, a natural and healthy devotion to the 'mother's heart at the heart of God' centres upon Theotokos, or 'Mother of God' as Mary and her place in the scheme of things were formally defined by the Universal Church at the Council of Chalcedon in AD 451.

In Ireland, Mary is a common name for girls, but in the Irish spelling *Maire*. Only Mary the Mother of God is spelled *Muire*. And where the ancient Celtic languages are spoken, Jesus, the Son of God, is often referred to as *Mac Mhuire* (Irish) or *Mab Mair* (Welsh), in other words, 'Mary's Son'.

> *Jesu MacMary, at dawn-tide, the flowing,*
> *Jesu MacMary, at ebb-tide, the going,*
> *When our first breath awakes,*
> *Life's day when darkness takes,*
> *Merciful God of all, mercy bestowing.*
> *With us and for us be,*
> *Merciful Deity,*
> *Amen, eternally.*[15]

In the doctrine of the Assumption of the Blessed Virgin Mary, C.G. Jung saw a symbol of tremendous power and equilibrium which could help to restore a lost balance to a man-dominated, woman-denying society. The undefined belief goes back to the fourth or fifth centuries, both in the East and the West.

Unfortunately, but probably inevitably, an attempt to define a mystery is inclined to harden controversy where it exists and to create controversy where it does not. Nevertheless, in its symbolic meaning, quite apart from any historical or other content, the mystery of the Assumption proclaims at the heart of Christian devotion that:

There is mother's heart in the heart of God.

It is of significance that, in those Reformed Christian traditions in which the place of Mary is diminished and her Assumption – however it may be understood – denied, there is usually also to be found a deep suspicion of the intuitive faculty in mankind, and a suppression of the whole feminine principle.

THE ALL-EMBRACING NATURE OF CELTIC CHRISTIANITY

*I should like to have a great ale-feast for the
King of Kings; I should like the Heavenly Host
to be drinking it for all eternity.*

*I should like there to be Hospitality for their
sake; I should like Jesus to be here always.*

Ninth-century Irish[16]

A culture which naturally expresses devotion in
terms of a party is not one likely to suffer from
world-rejection or an unreal separation of religion
from life.

Celtic Christianity is essentially an embracing of
life in its totality. Everything is sacred for there
is no such thing as the 'secular'. Creation is good
and blessed and beloved of God. There is no rejec-
tion of women or of the feminine, and although it
would be unrealistic to suppose a total equilibrium
of masculine and feminine, the tendency of Celtic
culture inclined in that direction. Women were more
'liberated' than in many other cultures.

Late twentieth-century Western culture suffers from
the divorce of organized religion from the totality
of life; from the divorce of religion from science,
and their all-too-frequent enmity; from a tendency
towards world-rejection and obsession with 'original
sin' instead of 'original righteousness', and the substantial denial of the feminine.

The intuition, a 'feminine' faculty which makes
up half of human nature, is in some extreme cases
identified with evil, and considered the realm of the
devil and his angels!

In terms of the New Testament revelation of God
in and through Jesus Christ, these things are nothing
less than pathological. The Celtic Church and Celtic
Christianity, as we are able to rediscover it, will help
us towards a wholeness and an equilibrium which,

in the West at any rate, has been lacking since long before the Reformation and increasingly seriously lacking ever since.

In the pages which follow, the causes of these dolours will be investigated, and their cures indicated. But Celtic Christianity is not a subject for religious archeology; it is a living and ever-present strand within the Churches which must urgently be rediscovered and restored to its proper place and perspective.

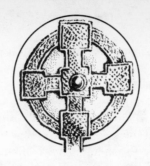

2·WHO ARE THESE PEOPLE?

Are you people in Galatia mad?
Has someone put a spell on you . . . ?

Galatians 3:1

Some ten years after the Second World War a Polish friend told me an extraordinary story. When Poland collapsed in 1939 he had made his way to France, via Romania; and when France fell the following year he escaped again to the United Kingdom. Polish army units were then reformed and based in Scotland.

My friend had no English, and so communication with local people presented great problems. However, his unit was soon posted to a location in the west Highlands and, to his astonishment, he discovered that as long as he confined himself to Polish and the local people confined themselves to Gaelic, they were able to enter into some kind of rough-and-ready communication.

He concluded that somehow, at some time, there must have been a common ancestry to Celt and Slav!

During the two or three millennia before Christ, Europe was populated by successive waves of incomers from central Asia or from across the Russian steppes. The process continued into the Christian era, but during the millennium immediately before

18

the birth of Jesus Christ, the northern neighbours of ancient Greece and Rome were known to them by the description, *Keltoi*, or 'strangers'.

A southern flank of this incoming wave had come south of the Black Sea and had settled in that part of modern Turkey known in Biblical times as Galatia. St Paul, justly exasperated with many of his fledgeling Christian congregations, found the Galatians no exception. But we look in vain for specifically 'Celtic' traits in Paul's Epistle. He was writing, as always, to members of Jewish synagogues who had accepted Jesus as the promised Messiah. There would no doubt have been a few Celts in the congregation – those local adherents to the Jewish religion from whom the Church was soon to draw its main strength – but the 'Celticness' of these Celts is, alas, not at all evident in Paul's Epistle.

Perhaps it is just as well. It would be as unwise to speculate about possible similarities between the Galatians and, let us say, the Welsh as it would be to equate the Pole with the west Highland Scot. And this kind of temptation is a real one, for romanticism abounds where things Celtic are discussed. In any consideration of Celtic Christianity and its relevance to the end of our twentieth century, romanticism must be avoided like the very plague!

CELTIC HISTORICAL ORIGINS

I see battle: a blond man
with much blood about his belt
and a hero-halo round his head.
His brow is full of victories.

A noble countenance I see,
working effect on womenfolk;
a young man of sweet colouring;
a form dragonish in the fray.

> He towers on the battlefield
> in breastplate and red cloak . . .
>
> The Tain[1]

It was Fedelm, the poetess of Connacht, who had this vision of Cuchulainn, and though the country was Ireland, the Greek historian Diodorus knew the vision well. Of the Celtic warriors threatening the Mediterranean civilizations, he wrote:

> Their aspect is terrifying . . . They are very tall in stature, with rippling muscles under clear, white skin. Their hair is blonde, but not naturally so: they bleach it, to this day, artificially, washing it in lime and combing it back from their foreheads . . . Some are clean-shaven, but others – especially those of high rank – shave their cheeks but leave a moustache that covers the whole mouth . . . The way they dress is astonishing: they wear brightly coloured and embroidered shirts, with trousers called *bracae* and cloaks fastened at the shoulder with a brooch . . . striped or chequered in design, with the separate checks close together and in various colours.
>
> The Celtic way of fighting was alarming. They wore: . . . bronze helmets with figures picked out on them, even horns, which make them look even taller than they already are . . . while others cover themselves with breast-armour made out of chains. But most content themselves with the weapons nature gave them: they go naked into battle.[2]

However, that broad spectrum of tribal groupings which made up the people whom we now refer to as Celts were very far from being savages. Archeology has revealed to us a Celtic civilization of no mean sophistication, whose crafts and artifacts are remarkable for the richness of their ornamentation, their subtlety and also their humour.

But, alas, we are almost entirely dependent upon the relatively new science of archaeology for any study of Celtic origins, for theirs was a heroic society with an oral tradition. They left behind no great cities – they were not city-dwellers – no inscriptions, and no documents for us to read for they were not a literate people until either colonized by Rome or converted to the Christian Faith. It was, for example, the Irish Christian monks who actually wrote down the ancient pagan legends such as the *Tain Bo Cuailange*.

Three principal archeological finds – those at Hallstatt in Austria, Hochdorf in Bavaria, and La Tene in Switzerland – have revealed a civilization of steadily developing sophistication. The period covered is between 800 BC (the primary Hallstatt date) and 100 BC (the latest La Tene date), with a very Cuchulainn-like chieftain's burial mound at Hochdorf from about 550 BC, revealing a quite astonishing splendour and flamboyance. The afterlife provisions in many respects recall those of ancient Egypt, and suggest a developed religious belief of some sophistication.

Sophisticated it might have been, but their afterlife provision was also endearingly human. A bronze cauldron containing the remains of five hundred litres of fermented honey-mead stood in a corner of the funerary chamber, and on the walls hung a row of fine, ornamented drinking-horns. The Celts believed in parties in their heaven!

For several centuries before Christ, the Celt was the terror of both Greece and Rome, but his was a tribal culture incapable of uniting to confront a disciplined and organized enemy. The Continental Celt was inexorably colonized and incorporated into the spreading Roman Empire. Hallstatt, Hochdorf and La Tene reveal a common Celtic heritage, but it is to the most far-flung of the Celtic peoples that we must confine our study.

IRISH CELTIC MYTHOLOGY

All below the ground was given to the Danaans.
They still live down there, spirits beneath the earth;
they still have their magic and they still practise their wizardry and tell stories drawn from the memories of the old days.
F. Delaney, *Legends of the Celts*[3]

Alone among the Celtic lands, Ireland escaped the attentions of Imperial Rome, and the heroic tribal culture survived more or less intact until the time of the Reformation. The Celtic Church completed and fulfilled the best of the old religion – the highly literate Irish monks preserved the old legends faithfully and committed them to writing, and the Celtic mind was not unduly troubled by the imposed mental processes of other cultures.

Even today all is not yet lost. Delaney reminds us that

the Irish ... teach as history the existence of an ancestral people who cast spells and made magic; the race of Dana, a goddess.

It comes naturally to the Celt to look to mythology rather than to history for his origins. There is more to this than meets the modern eye, for a myth has been aptly defined as 'a metaphor transparent to transcendence'. The ancestral myths may or may not point with more or less accuracy to historical events, but they do point to the underlying self-understanding of a people. They also serve to rationalize the current *status quo*. Thus the twelve sons of Israel were almost certainly the patriarchal

22

figures of twelve tribes, woven into a mythological common ancestry to give grounding to a twelve-tribe confederation.

Myth transcends historical events; it enshrines their meaning, and the self-perceived meaning of the people themselves.

A succession of mythological invasions settled in Ireland. The first inhabitants, related to Noah, died in the flood – all but one man (the hand of the Christian monk is discernible here). The next arrivals sailed in from the Atlantic and found themselves perpetually at war with evil and shapeless beings, the Formorians. All but one of these new arrivals died in a plague.

The remnant of a great fleet, lost at sea to the west, then arrived under their leader, Nemed. The Nemedians were eventually vanquished and driven out by the evil spirits. One, whose name was Britan, fled to the neighbouring isle and gave it its name. Others fled to – of all places – Greece, from whence they later returned under the name of the Fir Bolg (whom it is tempting to identify with the Belgae, a Celtic people who migrated to Britain a few centuries before Christ).

The Fir Bolg were joined and, one supposes, absorbed by new arrivals, also descended from the routed Nemedians, who:

> came in from the isles of the North, not in boats or marching over land but wafting purposefully through the air as an army of spirits, alighting softly on the fields on the first day of May. They called themselves the Tuatha de Danaan, the people of the goddess Danu.[4]

At the legendary Second Battle of Moytura, the power of the evil Formorians was broken and the Danaans entered into a golden age.

Finally, and also on the first of May, tall and beautiful warriors landed in the south-west. They

*The Man, symbol of St. Matthew. Gospel of
St. Matthew. Book of Kells.*

had sailed from Spain and, after several battles, they divided Ireland with the Tuatha de Danaan. The new arrivals – the Celts – were to live above the ground and the Danaan were to live beneath the earth, an arrangement which has proved satisfactory to the present day! And why not, indeed?

But how does archeology relate to this mythological framework? It seems clear that the first Celtic tribes came to Ireland in the Hallstatt period, speaking the older of two closely related Celtic languages, 'Q-Celtic' or Goidelic and, from Ireland, they invaded Britain from the west.

These invaders appear to have been driven back to Ireland by Celts coming directly from the Continent in the La Tene period, whose language was a later development, 'P-Celtic' or Brythonic. The Brythonic-speakers also invaded Ireland at a late stage but appear to have been absorbed into the Goidelic-speaking majority.

Thus we find the Goidelic languages in Ireland and the Isle of Man (and in Scotland by much later invasions); and the Brythonic in Wales, Cornwall and Brittany. Some at least of the the Picts of northern Scotland also seem to have spoken a form of P-Celtic.

It is interesting to discover that the original Q-Celtic speakers appear to have indeed arrived from Spain.

The mythology enshrines folk-memories concerning ancient migrations and arrivals. Equally importantly, it enshrines the meaning of things and establishes a sense of direction. It explains things, it establishes ancestry, it provides images for the tribal archetypes, often in the form of historical persons whose lives have been subjected to generations of heroic embroidery. Not least, it provides a framework within which aboriginal peoples – or the memories of them – can be set.

The mythology also comes to terms with that 'other' side of human experience: the reality of evil, the experience of psychically perceived phenomena and the fact of magic, however it may be understood. It is interesting to speculate upon the Tuatha de Danaan in their underground world. To what did they give a rational framework?

THE CELTS IN MAINLAND BRITAIN

*One dawn, Pwyll of Dyfed, lord of seven
hundred families, went hunting . . .*
F. Delaney, *Legends of the Celts*[5]

The Celtic settlement of mainland Britain probably took several centuries and was not, as popularly imagined, accomplished by sudden and catastrophic invasion. Successive waves of immigrants settled and either absorbed the existing folk or were absorbed by them. The over-population of France in the fifth century BC, which sent a Celtic horde through Italy to sack Rome in 387 BC, almost certainly provoked another significant influx into Britain from the Continent. Others were to follow.

Brythonic, or P-Celtic speaking Celts had absorbed whatever others there may have been by the beginning of the Roman colonization. The culture was the same, however: oral, heroic, tribal and above all, rural.

The effect of Roman colonization upon this culture was fundamental and catastrophic, for the Mediterranean culture of Rome was essentially urban. Towns were built, efficient communications were established and, in the course of time, the British Celt was either urbanized or turned into a tenant-farmer (if not actually a slave) by villa-dwelling Roman, or Romano-British country squires and grandees. In no time at all the well-to-do Briton was more Roman than the Romans!

Rome, her urban culture, her disciplined army, her forts and her roads, effectively obliterated the old way of life, just as she effectively obliterated the Druidic oral custodianship of tradition and lore. Celtic gods became as Romanized as their worshippers, a literate society, succeeded a non-literate society, and only fragments of the traditional culture survived, at the wild and mountainous fringes of the island.

The culture may have gone, but the people were the same, and the departure of the Romans, after some four hundred years, saw the rapid decay of towns and some kind of reversion to a rural tribalism. Irish invasions of western Wales and of Cornwall and Devon drove great numbers of P-Celts back to France where they revitalized the Celtic enclave of Brittany; but the Anglo-Saxon invasions put an end to any hope of a purely Celtic culture, by now predominantly Christian, being re-established in Britain.

In time, Celt and Anglo-Saxon intermingled and intermarried, united in a renewed Christian culture, and after the Danish invaders had finally been absorbed, the population of what was now England settled down to something like a common English identity.

Wales and Cornwall retained Celtic culture and language. Scotland up to the Clyde and some way beyond the Forth was absorbing the Anglo-Saxon; and north of the Highland line the Viking was battling with the Celt for supremacy, at least in the islands and along the western coastline. This last battle had several hundred years to run.

CELTIC PAGANISM

He is coming, Adzed-Head
on the wild-headed sea
with cloak hollow-headed
and curve-headed staff.

27

> *He will chant false religion*
> *at a bench facing East*
> *and his people will answer*
> *'Amen, Amen!'*
>
> Irish verse[6]

The Indo-European civilizations share a common religious heritage: Greeks, Romans and Celts worshipped a pantheon of gods whose origins are common with the gods of the Shivite tradition of contemporary Hinduism. As a heroic tribal people, the Celts seem to have made no serious attempt to represent their gods anthropomorphically in terms of statues and bas-reliefs until the beginning of the Christian era. Indeed it is said of the Celtic warrior, Brennus, that he laughed out loud at the Delphic statues of the Greek gods, wondering how anyone could be so foolish as to imagine gods could be like that!

The names of several gods and goddesses are known, but they help us little. Several of them were known by a number of different names, representing their different aspects or reflecting different tribal traditions. There is an interweaving of the gods with the heroes of mythology, and the legends of the heroes are inextricably bound up with Celtic religion, and for the most obvious of reasons.

Religion is about the meaning of existence. The Celtic heroes are archetypal images and thus they express something of the Celt's self-understanding and his experience of life. In this connection it is worth noting that most of them are tragic heroes and that sorrow is an underlying theme in a great many of them, of which *The Children of Turenn*, *The Children of Lir* and *The Children of Usna* – featuring Deirdre of the Sorrows – come most readily to mind.

The pagan Celt inhabited a living landscape. His was a culture lived as much on the psychical as on the physical level – elemental and nature spirits, spirits of river and mountain, of tree and stone, would have stood perpetually upon the frontiers of his perception. It is probable that the fine distinction between Creator and Creation may never have been fully made and so the propitiation of God the Creator (however understood), of archetypal and elemental forces, and of the water sprite in the nearby well, may have taken place at only haphazardly distinguishable levels.

I remember an incident in Malaya in the 1950s when the labour force building a new road downed tools and refused point-blank to fell a certain tree in the path of the road-trace. It was maintained that an important spirit inhabited that particular tree, and so the Works Department contracted with the local *Bomoh*, or shaman, to propitiate the spirit and persuade it to move house. This he did, with the appropriate offerings and magic, whereupon the labourers felled the first tree without a qualm.

As a brash young army officer, just posted to the mysterious East, I found the incident highly amusing. But why? And who was I to tell them that they were mistaken? One thing is certain – they had better manners than I had!

As in contemporary Hinduism, so possibly in pagan Druidism, the sophisticated may have seen in the gods various sub-personalities of the one God. The unsophisticated may have taken a different view, but we do not know for there is nobody to tell us.

Pre-Christian religion is concerned that Nature should keep on working, that the crops should grow, wives and cattle be fertile, and the elements remain in order. Ritual celebrations of symbolic and sympathetic magic naturally ensue, and of many variations both in tone and character.

Among the American Indians, only the Pawnee practised human sacrifice, and that of a single maiden (suitably kidnapped) once a year to the morning star. By contrast, their cousins in Mexico, whose religion was highly developed and heavily institutionalized, slaughtered hundreds at a time to the grotesque representations of their apparently insatiable gods. Archeology has not, however, revealed any evidence of involuntary human sacrifice in the British Isles earlier than the Iron Age.

We do not know how uniform Celtic religious practice was. The only sources are the propagandist accounts of Roman historians. They detail many gory rituals supposedly presided over by the Druids who naturally get a very bad press from the colonial power which was eager to slaughter them.

In fact we know very little about the Druids. There is evidence to suggest that they were not so much a priesthood as a caste in society associated with spiritual responsibilities, much as are the Brahmins of Hinduism. They probably combined a number of functions to which we can, at least to some degree, relate.

They were the custodians of the orally transmitted lore and tradition. They were 'wise' in perhaps the same way as the Chinese *Feng-shui sin-sang* (geomancer, shaman and popular psychologist!) is wise – as 'professors of cosmic harmony', relating people and their intentions to the subtle forces of the environment.

They were also *Bomohs*, shamans or witch-doctors, with knowledge of the inner dynamics of things and of the magic that would manipulate them for good or for ill.

They were the medicine-men, revered, like the famous Sioux Indian Sitting Bull, more for their skill with elemental and nature forces, their wisdom and their healing, than for any prowess on the battlefield. They were sorcerers, magicians, priests. They were men of power on every level and thus subject to all the possibilities of corruption that psychic power in particular can bring. There would have been among them both good men and bad, according to their lights. More than this is mere speculation.

Of the ordinary, everyday character, experience and

beliefs of the pagan Celt we can only speculate. It is certain that religion and life would have been one and the same thing, but of the moral content of religion, of the self-understanding of the pagan Celt in the sight of God, and of his ultimate hope, we know next to nothing other than the hints that archeology has given us.

There is the notion, widespread if not universal in the pagan world, of a doctrine of reincarnation in Druidism, and also a suggestion of some kind of messianic hope. One of the many Columban traditions has it that Saint Columba appealed to this very hope and announced its fulfilment in Christ upon his arrival on the Druidic Holy Isle of Iona. It is a nice story, and profoundly Pauline in its approach, but it may or may not be true.

It seems clear beyond very much doubt, however, that there was a cruel, demonic element in Celtic paganism. A religion of propitiation is in any event a religion of fear, of psychic dread, and it may be of significance that there was no Celtic goddess of love.

It was to such a people as we have described, with a religious background which we must reconstruct from fragments by intelligent guesswork, that the Christian Faith first came with the Roman Army by the end of the first century AD. It spread with remarkable rapidity and reached Ireland by the early fifth century at the latest. It is to the conversion of the Celt to the Christian Faith, and to the nature of that Faith, that we must now turn.

3·THE FAITH AMONG THE BRITONS

His name was almost certainly not Amphibalus. That was the name of his cloak! But it is as Amphibalus that he is remembered, and his date is now generally held to have been a century earlier than that given by Gildas, the Celtic historian, and Bede the Anglo-Saxon.

Amphibalus was a Christian priest, exercising his ministry in or near the important Roman town of Verulamium at the end of the second century or the very beginning of the third. His church would have been a private house to which the Faithful came. There may possibly have been more than one house, and he may have had a number of small, scattered ecclesia to serve. He would also have had a secular job – his priesthood would have been known only to his fellow-Christians and, at that period in British history, of relevance only within the context of the Faithful.

Amphibalus would have been a member of a College of *Presbyteroi*, or priests, of whom the chief would have been the *episcopus* or bishop. Quite where his *episcopus* was based is not known to us, but by the end of the second century there would have have been several bishops in Britain, based in the towns, with Metropolitans (whom we would now call archbishops) ruling the Church from the centres of the Roman Prefectures.

The Faith came to Britain with the Romans. In spite of the Christian abhorrence of military service, there were Christian soldiers in units of the Roman Army. Merchants, administrators, colonists of all kinds, arrived and quickly established the Roman rule all over what we now know as England and, less securely, into parts of Wales and southern Scotland. Every kind of Mediterranean religious cult would have come with them. The pagan gods were quickly identified with the local Celtic pantheon, but the various Greek mystery religions were soon very much in vogue, and the cult of Mithras was very strong, particularly in the Army.

The Christian Faith may well have seemed, at first, to be yet another of the new mystery religions, but, unlike them, it quickly revealed itself to be all-embracing and everyone-embracing. It spoke of mankind loved with an everlasting love, of God the Creator taking human nature to Himself – and of the cost of it – and all for love's sake. It spoke of forgiveness, integrity and eternal life. It swept up the best of paganism in an all-fulfilling embrace, and revealed Creation as the transfigured image of God.

The Christian Faith was not, however, entirely respectable. It was suspected of political unreliability and from time to time there would be an outbreak of persecutions.

The common dedicatory phrase, *Numina Augustorum* ('To the Divine Presences of the Emperors') was anathema to Christians who, in common with Jews, would not burn incense to representations of the Emperor as was expected of all loyal citizens. The Jews were officially exempt, and as the Christian Faith could, at a pinch, be regarded as a form of Judaism, this piece of formal – almost meaningless – pagan conformism was not always demanded of them.

But sometimes it was, and as a matter of official policy. It was death to refuse under these circumstances, and Christians had to keep a very low profile in times of official persecution.

Amphibalus became a hunted man either under the persecution of Septimus Severus (c.209), or possibly under Decius (c.254). (The even later date of c.305 given by Gildas and Bede is now generally discounted.) In either event, this suggests to us a settled, well-established Christian Church before the beginning of the third century. Its numerical strength may have been relatively small, and it was probably very scattered, but it was there, and operating. In the famous expression of Teilhard de Chardin, it was 'Omega, present and operating at the core of the thinking mass'.

Amphibalus was hidden by a sympathetic Roman soldier named Albanus. Albanus became a Christian in the course of their association and enabled the priest's escape by dressing himself in the priest's cloak. He was seized, confessed the Christian Faith, and was executed for it. He has given Verulamium its present name of St Albans.

'SEU GENTILIS SEU CRISTIANUS'

The attendance-list of a great Council of Bishops, held at Arles in France in 314, records the arrival of the Celtic Romano-British, Bishops of London, Lincoln and York. At about this time, Annianus, a supplicant of the goddess Sulis Minerva at the great temple of Aqua Sulis in Bath, wrote a request to the goddess on a strip of lead, as was the custom. Annianus sought the return of some silver coins which had been stolen from him, and asked the goddess to recover the money from the thief *seu gentilis seu cristianus* ('whether pagan or Christian'). The Christian Faith was no doubt widespread by this time, but it was by no means universal, nor was it necessarily fashionable, or even popular.

The Christian Faith had become *religio licita* – an officially permitted religion – in the year 260, notwithstanding which some further, quite severe, persecutions were to ensue.

When the Roman Commander-in-Chief in York, Constantius Chlorus, became Emperor in 292, his wife Helen had long been a Christian believer. Constantius was succeeded, in the year 306, by their son, Constantine, also a believer, though like his mother, as yet unbaptized. Helen received baptism in 312, and the following year the Christian Faith was granted official Imperial favour. By the year 313 the Christian Faith had been in Britain for some two hundred years but it was now possible for Christians to build churches as centres for their worship.

Several early Romano-British church foundations survive. Caerlean-on-Usk has one, and the present church of Saint Mary-de-Lode in Gloucester is built on the foundations of another – itself built into the ruins of an earlier villa. In Gloucestershire alone, the important Anglo-Saxon church of Deerhurst-on-Severn is built over a late Romano-British church; and churches at Ozleworth, Hewelsfield and Oldbury-on-Severn are also probably originally Romano-British Christian foundations.

Nearer to St Albans, the ancient church at Ippollitts near Hitchin is dedicated to the Romano-British Saint Hippolytus. Archeology also reveals to us a growing evidence of Romano-British Christian cemeteries, both urban and rural. A Faith centred upon the Resurrection, and with an urgent eschatological hope, was inclined to be particular about the niceties of burial, and archeologists appear to have had little difficulty in identifying such sites as have been found.

While the Christians in Britain were building their

first churches, the Universal Church was shaken by a popular heresy advanced by an Alexandrian priest by the name of Arius. An entirely new, political dimension to doctrinal dispute was experienced in that Arianism was at one stage taken up by the Imperial Court and, very briefly, declared official! Arianism denied the Divine Nature in Christ, and portrayed Jesus as the 'Demiurge', or heavenly superman. This was conceived as a *created* being of whom an Arian hymn proclaimed:

There was when he was not!

Britain does not seem to have been particularly affected by the Arian controversy which was condemned at the great Council of Nicea in 325, but it was a British lay monk, Pelagius (whose Celtic name was Morgan), who was to provoke the next doctrinal uproar. In the first place he objected, not unreasonably, to some statements in the *Confessions* of Saint Augustine of Hippo, but was then in all probability pushed altogether too far in subsequent arguments with Augustine himself. We shall encounter the redoubtable Augustine on a later page. For the moment it is sufficient to note that Pelagianism, the suggestion that man has no need of Divine Grace, was refuted in Britain by means of a campaign in 429 by Bishops Germanus of Auxerre and Lupus of Troyes from whom the British hierarchy asked assistance.

A little while before Pelagius achieved his notoriety and about the year 389, a son was born to Concessa, the wife of a Romano-British Christian deacon by the name of Calpurnius. Calpurnius was also a *decurion*, the holder of an obligatory civil office and thus in all probability a Roman citizen of some standing. His own father, Potitus, had been a Christian priest.

Calpurnius, Concessa and their son lived at Banna venta Bernia, and the likeliest candidate for such a name is the Roman wall fort of Birdoswald in

Cumbria. Bernia may refer to the nearby Greenhead Pass (British *bern* = mountain pass). The boy had two names, one was Magonus, and the other – the one by which he is known to the world – Patrick.

We shall return to Patrick on a later page, but it is sufficient for the present to note that his father, a man of standing in the community, was a Christian deacon and that his grandfather had been a priest. If Potitus had been, let us say, fifty years of age when young Patrick was born, he himself being in all likelihood brought up in Christian surroundings, then we are left with a picture of a well-established local Church from at least 313 if not considerably before.

It may be no accident that a substantial number of ancient church foundations, especially in the north, are dedicated to Saint Helen, the much loved wife of the one-time C-in-C, Roman Army, York.

By the time of Patrick's birth, the Roman Empire was under great strain and was in places beginning to break up under the pressures, internally, of demoralization and corruption and, externally, from a fresh tide of incoming tribes from the east.

Britain began to be raided by Germanic pirates from the Continent. By the time young Patrick had reached his twenties, the Roman Army had been withdrawn altogether and Britain was left to fend for itself but without the resources, or the training, to do so. The cities began to decay, the fabric of society began to fall apart, internecine warfare broke out, and Germanic mercenaries were hired to protect the disorganized Britons from Germanic tribal invasion.

It was a recipe for calamity. Angles, Saxons and Jutes poured into the country, many of their leaders taking over the old Roman estates, complete with Celtic tenants and bondsmen. The incomers were pagans, and large numbers of nominally Christian Celts reverted to paganism. The collapsing Romano-British, Celtic and by now largely Christian, culture was pushed further and further westwards.

Their Church was to be severely criticized for not evangelizing the Anglo-Saxon invaders effectively, but with the whole fabric of life in disarray, and the culture of three hundred safe and comfortable years breaking up all about them, it is perhaps more surprising that they held their ground as well as they did.

EARLY CELTIC EVANGELISM

I traced the sign of the cross
which St Samson, with his own hand,
carved by means of an iron instrument
on a standing stone.

K. M. Evans[1]

The monastic life, a feature of the Christian Church from as early as the second century, was established in Britain by the end of the fourth. There has always been a temptation to project later, medieval forms of monasticism back into the early Christian period, and this can be profoundly misleading. Nevertheless, the monastery, however understood, became an important feature of Celtic Christianity.

Gildas (c.500–c.570) was a monk and the first British historian. According to the earliest accounts of him, Gildas was born in Strathclyde but was forced to take refuge in Wales where, after the death of his young wife, he came under the influence of Illtud, a former soldier, now leader of a community at Llantwit Major.

Gildas wrote his history, *De Excidio et Conquestu Brittaniae*, over many years. It is cumbersome and verbose and, its whole purpose being horatory, its value as history is strictly limited. Gildas gives exaggerated accounts of the ills of the day, blaming them squarely upon the failures of the British rulers, secular and ecclesiastical.

It is Gildas who tells us of the incursions, both of

the Picts in the north, and of the Irish into Wales, at the beginning of the fifth century. At the same time the Germanic raids were causing great anxiety and it was an 'arrogant usurper', whom Bede identifies as Wortigernos, who made the classic mistake of hiring Germanic mercenaries to fight off Germanic invaders.

Gildas goes on to tell of a later, legitimate British ruler, Ambrosius Aurelianus, leading a revival of British fortunes which culminated in the decisive victory over the Anglo-Saxons at Mount Badon close to the year 500. Gildas does not mention the *Dux*, or military commander, Arthur, who became a legend in his own lifetime with his twelve victories, and who passed into immortality identified with the principal archetypal image of the British mythology.

Two hill forts, one in Wiltshire and one in Dorset, are the least unlikely sites of Mount Badon, and here it is of interest that Britain west of this general area seems to have been the last part to been evangelized. Few traces of the Christian Faith are found here which are earlier than the sixth century.

The late fifth and sixth centuries saw considerable evangelistic activity in the west country, mostly from south Wales. Pressure from the Irish raids, however, produced a steady stream of emigration from Devon and Cornwall to Armorica on the French coast, the incoming Britons giving it a new name, Brittany.

The great evangelist bishop, Samson of Dol, like Gildas a pupil of Illtud, did most of his work first in Cornwall and then in Brittany. In both places the work of evangelization was done by implanting small communities of Christians (later described as monasteries, but how 'monastic' in a later sense is unclear) from the security of which the surrounding countryside could be covered. It was a feature of all the Celtic Churches that their evangelistic and pastoral work was based upon communities living the life of worship and contemplation from which evangelists could go out and to which they could return.

The Anglo-Saxons, securely settled east of the Pennines, and indeed down to the Sussex coast and as far west as Hampshire, intermingled with the indigenous Celts, intermarried, and remained pagan. That Christians remained in the paganized east seems almost certain, but they were cut off from the life of the Church to which they had belonged.

Towards the end of the sixth century, Anglo-Saxon invasions of the west began to take place. In 577, Ceawlin and Cutha, with the war-host of Wessex, defeated the British at Dyrham, near Bristol. Three local Celtic kings fell in battle, and their towns of Cirencester, Bath and Gloucester fell into Anglo-Saxon hands. Among those killed at Dyrham was Eldad (or Aldate), a bishop, possibly of Gloucester.

At about the same time, Chester also fell to a thrust from the north-east, and so Wales was isolated and the remaining British Church and culture was broken into three fragments: Lancashire and Cumbria, Wales, and Cornwall. The local British dialects began to split into separate languages at this time, and of Cumbrian Celtic only a few place names and the names of mountains (eg: Helvelyn and Blencathra) now remain.

Paradoxically, it is among the Anglo-Saxons of the mid-seventh century, and on their long-time settled east coast, that we find the 'Celtic Church' and 'Celtic Christianity' drawn vividly to our attention. For it was in the Anglo-Saxon kingdoms of Elmet and Northumbria that the Celtic missionaries from Ireland met, and clashed significantly with, the claims and demands of the missionaries from Rome.

THE ARRIVAL OF AUGUSTINE

If Augustine is meek and lowly of heart, it shows that he bears the yoke of Christ himself, and offers it to you. But if he is haughty and

unbending, then he is not of God, and you should
not listen to him.

Bede, *History of the English Church
and People*[2]

It was, perhaps, five hundred years after the first
Christian believers arrived to settle in Britain that
the Prior of the Monastery of St Andrew, in Rome,
landed in Kent to be warmly welcomed by the
Kentish King Ethelbert at Canterbury. He was given
every encouragement to preach the Christian Faith
and, within a few months, it was formally adopted
for the Kentish Kingdom. Ethelbert's wife, Bertha,
was already a Christian and it seems that there was
the makings of a congregation ready and waiting.

Augustine did not, therefore, enter into a vacuum
as far as the Faith was concerned, nor had he been
sent into one. Pope Gregory, stirred by the sight of
Anglian slaves in Rome, had sent his lieutenant
primarily to take charge of the British Church and
to stir it into a more vigorous evangelism of the still
pagan Anglo-Saxons.

Having established his Kentish base, Augustine
then returned as far as Arles in order to be consecrated Bishop. He then took up his new post, that of
Archbishop of Canterbury.

The mantle of the Roman Emperors had fallen upon
the shoulders of the Bishops of Rome. The Church of
the Western Patriarch was imperialist through and
through, but in all probability this was largely an
unconscious phenomenon. The Bishop of Rome was
the successor of Saint Peter (though it is doubtful if
the Apostle would ever have thought of himself as 'of
Rome'!) and, just as imperial authority had proceeded
from the Emperor, so now, ecclesiastical authority
proceeded from the Pope. It was a very natural habit
of reasoning into which to fall, and few questioned it.

It did, however, impart a style which was to prove
unhelpful. A first meeting with British clerics had

proved unsatisfactory. Augustine had been imperious and had demanded that the British Church adapt their customs forthwith to Roman norms. A second meeting was arranged a few weeks later when a delegation of seven bishops, attended by a number of other learned clerics, set out from the ancient monastery of Bangor in north Wales to meet Augustine. There were a number of issues to be discussed, including the correct calculation of the date of Easter, but central to them all was the question of their submission to his authority as papally appointed Archbishop and Primate. How were they to deal with him honestly and in a truly Christian manner? On their way they sought the advice of an anchorite of known wisdom and sanctity: 'If Augustine is a man of God, follow him!'

But how were they to know this? The anchorite gave the advice quoted at the head of this section and added: 'If he rises courteously as you approach, rest assured that he is the servant of Christ and do as he asks. But if he ignores you and does not rise, then, since you are in the majority, do not comply with his demands.'

Augustine received his Celtic brothers-in-Christ coldly and arrogantly, and he remained seated. They then accused him of a pride which made nonsense of his claims. He became angry and blustering and then tried to compromise, but it was too late. He had forfeited both their confidence and their respect. They departed, saying that as he declined to rise to greet his brethren in the first instance he would have scant respect for them once they submitted to his authority.

In one important respect, however, the Celts were out of their depth. Authority was not what it had seemed to be – the true name of the game was *power*, and this was a category which had not entered into their calculations at all.

DIVISIONS BETWEEN CELTIC AND ROMAN CHRISTIANITY

The only people who are stupid enough to disagree with the whole world are these Scots and their obstinate adherents the Picts and Britons, who inhabit only a portion of these two islands in a remote ocean!

Bede, *History of the English Church and People*[3]

One of Augustine's most faithful companions in Kent was Paulinus, who had been sent by the Pope in 601 to reinforce the Kentish mission. In 625, Ethelburga of Kent married Edwin, the pagan King of Northumbria, and Paulinus travelled north with her where, two years later, Edwin and his chiefs accepted the Christian Faith and were baptized. In 633 Edwin was defeated and killed by the pagan chieftain Cadwallon, and Paulinus returned to Kent with Queen Ethelburga, where he became Bishop of Rochester.

The sons of Ethelfrith, an earlier Northumbrian king displaced by Edwin in 616, had fled to Scotland, and Oswald, the eldest surviving, had been converted to the Christian Faith by the Irish monks on Iona. When Edwin was killed Oswald returned to claim his kingdom. He defeated and killed Cadwallon and sent to Iona for help to establish the Christian Faith in Northumbria all over again.

After one false start, the Iona community sent Bishop Aidan to Northumbria with some companions, and they were given the Isle of Lindisfarne as the base for their operations, the King himself taking part in the work of evangelism. After seven years, Oswald was defeated and killed near the Welsh border by Penda the pagan King of Mercia. The work went on, however, and Lindisfarne quickly became established as a centre, not merely of evangelism, but of a transparent holiness as well.

The Church, as established by the Irish monks in Northumbria, differed from the Church on the

Continent in a very few matters. Liturgically there was no significant difference but, among the Irish Christians, ecclesiastical oversight was by the abbot of the controlling monastery who might or might not be a bishop. If not, then one of his monks was in bishop's orders and fulfilled the bishop's liturgical functions for him.

There were some differences in trivialities, such as the style of clerical tonsure. The Roman tonsure involved the shaving of the crown of the head, while the Celtic (possibly following Druid custom) appears to have involved shaving the front of the head – or part of it – forward of a line from ear to ear.

There was also an awkward difference when it came to calculating the date of Easter. There had been much controversy over this in the fourth and fifth centuries, but the Alexandrian practice was formally adopted by Rome in 525. The Celtic Churches had adopted their own methods of calculation and had fallen out of step in this respect with standardized Continental practice.

It was the disagreement on this issue between the Roman mission coming up from Kent, and the Irish mission moving down from Lindisfarne, that occasioned the Synod of Whitby in 664. Oswy, King of Northumbria, was Irish in observance, but his Queen Eanfleda was Roman. They therefore seldom observed Easter together, for the Celtic Church had its own method of determining the 'Paschal Moon' which was different from the Roman. There was at that period no one generally accepted method throughout Christendom. Their domestic confusion was indicative of a wider and more damaging confusion, and a synod was called to discuss the matter.

Bishop Colman of Lindisfarne, with the King himself, headed the Irish delegation and explained their usage as agreeable to the teachings of the apostle John, and deriving from the usage of Columba of Iona, the apostle of Scotland.

The Roman delegation was headed by one Agilbet, but his spokesman was a Northumbrian priest by the name of Wilfred who was more Roman than the Pope! He was a clever young man who spoke in a haughty and contemptuous manner, ridiculing the Celts and their usage and pointing out that – apart from these abberants – the whole world followed Roman custom! He spoke slightingly of Columba and laid great stress on the authority of Saint Peter who was, after all, the keeper of the keys of heaven and of hell! Some of Wilfred's words head this section.

The real point at issue, once again, was *power* disguised as ecclesiastical authority. King Oswy ruled in favour of Rome for, 'as St Peter is guardian of the gates of heaven, I shall not contradict him!'

The Alexandrian calculations of Easter, and other minor Roman customs, were agreed and imposed upon the Church of what was now England by Archbishop Theodore in 669. The Lindisfarne community split, Bishop Coleman taking the Irish monks back to Ireland, while the English monks remained to make Northumbria briefly rival Byzantium as a centre of holiness and learning.

But to our generation something precious seems to have departed with the Irish monks. We have inclined to contrast the 'Celtic Church' with the Roman ever since, and to have wondered if 'their' version of the Christian Faith was not, in some way, purer and nearer to the source than our own.

Lest romanticism should seem to threaten, we must now attend, briefly, to the background from which Augustine of Canterbury came and to the cast of ecclesiastical mind which came with him. Thereafter we can return to look at the coming of the Faith to those other, and more continuingly and demonstrably Celtic, peoples of the British Isles.

4·THEOLOGICAL, PSYCHOLOGICAL — OR PATHOLOGICAL?

May an expectant mother be baptized? How soon after childbirth may she enter church? ... And may a woman enter church at certain periods? And may she receive Communion at these times? And may a man enter church after relations with his wife before he has washed? Or receive the sacred mystery of Communion? These uncouth English people require guidance on all these matters.

Bede, *History of the English Church and People*[1]

Immediately after his consecration as Bishop, and before returning to Kent, Augustine of Canterbury addressed a series of questions to Pope Gregory. The first seven are administrative and receive answers remarkable for their common-sense and pastoral sensitivity. The eighth question, most of which is reproduced above, is of a quite different character and provokes an answer as remarkable for its awkwardness as for its length.

Pope Gregory referred to the Old Testament teachings on these matters, and related them to the changed understandings of Christians. In what was essentially a pastoral – even liberal – approach, he reveals never-theless a somewhat curious attitude to the sexual expression of the love of husband and wife. 'The fault lies in the bodily desire ... the desire is in the bodily union.' And, more starkly:

> When a man's mind is attracted to these pleasures by lawless desire, he should not regard himself as fitted to join in Christian worship until these heated desires cool in the mind, and he has ceased to labour under wrongful passions.
>
> Bede, *History of the English Church and People*[2]

Pope Gregory was talking about husbands and wives! He went on to make it clear that the firm intention to procreate children was *the only lawful cause* for sexual intercourse between husband and wife. On no account must they *enjoy* their lovemaking!

When I first read Bede's reproduction of this letter, as a young subaltern in the early 1950s, I found it disturbing and well-nigh incredible. Forty years later, and with a better understanding of the background, I find it deeply distressing, even tragic.

What was Augustine bringing back with him on his joyful return to Kent as first Archbishop of Canterbury?

CELIBACY IN THE EARLY BRITISH CHURCH

I wish, O Son of the Living God, ancient eternal King, for a secret hut in the wilderness that it may be my dwelling.

A very blue shallow well to be beside it, a clear pool for washing away sins through the grace of the Holy Ghost.

*A beautiful wood close by around it on every
side, for the nurture of many-voiced birds, to
shelter and hide it.*

Tenth-Century Irish[3]

The life of contemplation, alone in a hermitage or
with brethren in a monastery, has been part of the
total life of the Church almost from the beginning. It
was to the desert that the first Christian contemplatives retired, as had Jesus Himself for a short while at
the beginning of His ministry. The desert was the only
wilderness available. The tenth-century Irish monk
quoted above was fortunate in having the beauty of
Creation all about him, Creation being to him the
transfigured image of the Creator.

Jesus made reference to those who 'have renounced
marriage for the sake of the Kingdom of Heaven.' The
context of this was a discussion on the responsibilities of husband and wife to each other.

The married state was most decidedly the normal
and expected one in Israel. The known celibates are
few indeed, perhaps only Jeremiah in the Old Testament, and Paul in the New. But Paul, writing to the
congregation in Corinth, advised against marriage in
the circumstances as they were then believed to be.
The Second Coming was believed to be imminent,
this was no time to enter into fresh complications!
(Paul, be it noted, was a bachelor!) But if they must
marry – go ahead! 'It is better to marry than to burn
(with unfulfilled desire)!'

The monastery was a powerful institution among
the Celts, certainly in Ireland, Scotland and Wales.
The assumption is generally made that these communities were celibate, and this was probably the
case. But was this invariable? The somewhat later
Abbots of Dunkeld were succeeded by their sons
for generations! To what extent, and under what
circumstances, therefore, were some 'monasteries'
more like a Christian version of a modern Israeli

kibbutz – a community of Christians in a still partly pagan countryside – than cenobitic monks in a true monastery?

In the eighth and ninth centuries, there was a tendency among solitary contemplatives in Ireland and Scotland to band together in groups of thirteen (suggestive of Christ and his twelve apostles). These, known as *Culdees* (Irish: *cele de*, meaning 'companions'), were at times fiercely critical of other communities and violently antagonistic to women. The reasons for this were probably more psychological than theological.

A fear of sex and of sexuality in general does not seem to have been a usual feature of the Church in the British Isles before the time of Augustine of Canterbury. Celibacy seems to have been a state entered into 'for the sake of the Kingdom of Heaven', as a man or woman's sense of vocation required. That the clergy should be celibate of necessity seems not to have been an issue.

In the Mediterranean world it was somewhat different. In the first place there had been a number of powerfully world-denying and falsely 'spiritualizing' influences from such movements as Gnosticism and Manichaeism from whose influence these islands seem to have escaped almost completely. Manichaeism taught that 'particles of light' had been stolen from Heaven by Satan and imprisoned in the human brain. The whole purpose of religion was to release these 'particles' back into the light. Asceticism and world-rejection featured strongly in the movement, and it shared with certain of the manifestations of Gnosticism (literally Esoteric Knowledge-ism) an abhorrence of 'the flesh'. In addition, there was a growing tradition of asceticism in the Mediterranean world – some of it pathological – and there was also the strongly celibate influence of the Desert Fathers.

The Council of Nicea in 325 rejected a proposition that clergy should give up cohabitation with their

The Lion, symbol of St. Mark. Gospel of St. Matthew.
Book of Kells.

wives. A number of Councils in the East specifically upheld the right of clergy to marry, and the Council of Trullo (named after the *trullus*, or domed hall, in the palace of Emperor Justinian II in Constantinople) in 692 finalized the matter. The Christian East has, ever since, chosen its bishops from those in monastic vows, but other clergy are free to marry before their ordination, though not after it.

In the West there was clearly a growing climate of opinion in favour of clerical celibacy, and attempts were made to enforce it as early as the Council of Elvira in 306. The inference was that the clergy 'ought' to renounce marriage for the sake of the Kingdom of Heaven. The clergy were in the process of becoming separated from the great body of the Faithful. Clericalism was taking hold, however unconsciously. The clergy were to be an elite, a *caste!*

Into this somewhat obsessed western Mediterranean climate was born at Carthage in 354, to a pagan father and a Christian mother, a child who was to grow up into one of the towering intellects of the Western Church. His influence for both good and ill was to be far-reaching and long-lasting.

The personal psychology of Saint Augustine of Hippo – for as such the Church knows him – is, I suggest, the root cause of our search for a more authentic experience of the Christian Gospel in 'Celtic Christianity' and the 'Celtic Church'.

AUGUSTINE OF HIPPO

There [in heaven] we shall rest and we shall see;
We shall see and we shall love;
We shall love and we shall praise.
Behold what shall be in the end and shall not end.

Saint Augustine of Hippo[4]

Saint Augustine of Hippo, some of whose words head this section, was a great man and a holy man to whom we are profoundly indebted; but like any other man, he was flawed. He was also tormented. His deep psychological problems coloured his theology and his torment-darkened theology was to have a profound effect upon the thinking processes of the whole Western Church. The effects are still with us today.

Augustine received a Christian education, but was not baptized into the Faith which he in any case abandoned at University. At the same time he took a mistress who remained faithful to him for fifteen years and bore him a son, Adeodatus. Augustine then became a Manichaean and moved, first to Rome and then to Milan, where he lectured in rhetoric.

At Milan, Augustine came under the influence of its bishop, Ambrose. He began to feel not only drawn back to the Christian Faith, which he had long since abandoned, but also to a life of monasticism of which Ambrose was a powerful advocate.

In 386 he dismissed his faithful mistress who returned to Africa broken-hearted. The following year he was baptized, and in 388 he returned to Africa and established a monastery at Tagaste. He was ordained priest in 391 and consecrated Bishop in 395.

Augustine was intellectually brilliant; it was perhaps the intellectual in him which defined Faith as 'Intellectual Assent' in spite of the Epistle to the Hebrews which says 'Faith gives assurance to our hopes, and makes us certain of realities we do not see.' He was widely educated, ardent and gifted with mystical insight, but he was also flawed. He was able to *specifically deny, in defiance of scripture, that women were made in the 'image and likeness of God'!*

Augustine was tormented with guilt, and his torment centred upon his own sexuality. It is easy for us to psychologize Augustine now, but it was impossible for him at that time. In his teachings *he specifically identified sex with sin*, but it was the controversy stirred up by the Briton, Pelagius, which was to provoke his most despairing and damaging outpourings.

Augustine interpreted the story of Adam and Eve quite literally. He saw the unfallen Adam as endowed with all possible wisdom and knowledge. As a result of Adam's disobedience, however, these attributes were entirely lost and henceforth, in Augustine's view, mankind suffers, from a hereditary moral disease – *sexually transmitted* – as a result of which he is under a 'harsh necessity' of commiting sin. In Augustine's view, not only is there an original sin but there is a continuing liability of original guilt that goes with it.

Augustine saw the whole human race as a *massa peccati* – a mass of sin – out of which God elects some fortunate souls to receive His quite unmerited mercy. He believed that infants, dying unbaptized, go to everlasting perdition. His guilt-ridden vision is characterized by an extreme pessimism on the one hand, and a wonder at the mercy of God and of the workings of His grace on the other. Augustine was obliged to develop such complex theories about the workings of God's grace that, when I wrestled with them as a theological student, I found myself hoping that God understood them and was managing to do all the right things!

There was a streak of cruelty in Augustine, discernible in many of his writings, and that his theology was psychologically conditioned is so obvious now that it hardly needs to be stated – at times it comes close to the pathological. It has been the great misfortune of the Western Church ever since that, at the time, the climate was ripe for its extensive – though never quite complete – adoption.

Fortunately, this tormented soul, whom the shallow-thinking Pelagius goaded into articulating such essentially unscriptural theological darkness, was not by any means all darkness within. In his *Confessio*, perhaps the first ever autobiography (and thus perhaps indicative of a deep, unconscious need to justify himself), he addressed God in words which are as true for every other human being as they were for himself:

> Thou hast made us for Thyself and our hearts
> are restless till they rest in Thee.[5]

THE DOCTRINE OF ORIGINAL SIN

> *There is a youth comes wooing me:*
> *O King of Kings, may he succeed!*
> *Would he were stretched upon my breast,*
> *with his body against my skin.*
> Isobel, Countess of Argyll (fifteenth-century)[6]

With a growing exaltation of celibacy as the proper state for a spiritual elite, an increasing clericalization of the Western Church, a concentration of power – identified with authority – at Rome, and the Pope assuming a spiritualized version of the imperial mantle, it is little wonder that the teachings of Augustine of Hippo found largely uncritical favour.

Pope Leo the Great (440–461) forbade married men to put away their wives upon ordination, but decreed that they were henceforth to live with them as brother and sister. Sex was too innately sinful to have anything to do with love, or for clergymen to so much as contemplate, even with their wives!

This was the background to Augustine of Canterbury's eighth question (and the ninth which followed it). And this was also the background against which Gregory's reply must be understood. An all-male teaching authority in the Church, celibate by compulsion and brought up to regard sex as sin, could only regard woman as a threat. All the makings of a grotesque, and – tragically – largely unconscious, distortion of the Gospel and of its its implications were thus to hand.

Henceforth there was always the danger of a schizoid separation of 'religion' from 'life'. Sexuality was now a subject quite unsuitable for prayer – other than in grovelling repentance with a sense of perpetual guilt! The early fifteenth-century prayer by Isobel, Countess of Argyll, to our Lord, the King of Kings, quoted at the head of this section, was either the prayer of a blasphemer – or that of a perfectly normal Celtic woman in love!

Perhaps most sadly of all, clerical concubinage, with all its degradation both of women in general and of the men who practised it, was to be a more or less winked-at perpetual scandal throughout the subsequent history of the Western Church.

We cannot be sure what the attitude of the British Church had been to these matters, nor can we be sure of the attitude of the Church in Ireland which was founded somewhat later. Links between Britain and the Continent were strong, but the various Mediterranean controversies passed these north Atlantic islands by. Perhaps the reaction of the Briton, Pelagius, to what he regarded as dehumanizing in Augustine's *Confessio*, may give us some indication. But Pelagius went – or more probably was driven – much too far in his arguments and was himself quite properly condemned for them.

The real mischief of Augustine's distorted vision and its too-ready acceptance at Rome was that he succeeded in removing the Church's gaze from the Blessed Creation, which God created good and which is the transfigured image of its Creator. Henceforth it would be fixed instead upon Adam's Fall and the doctrine of Original Sin.

Henceforth, *the whole interpretation of the Gospel began with Original Sin* (and not infrequently with the idea of transmitted guilt as well). The Blessed Creation slowly and inexorably began to be pushed to the outer fringes of Western theological sight and mind.

5·THE CONVERSION OF WALES, SCOTLAND AND IRELAND

When the spirit makes thin the canvas we see
that the universe is a creation.

Gwenallt[1]

The great Carthaginian theologian Tertullian wrote in about the year 208, concerning 'districts of the Britons, unreached by Romans, but subdued to Christ.' There is a distinct probability that he was referring to Wales.

Wales passed under Roman rule, but the country is mountainous and had a heroic tribal culture. Towns, such as they might have been, were few and far between. We know very little indeed about the Church in Wales until the time of Maxen Wledig.

In 383 Magnus Maximus (Maxen Wledig) rebelled against the Emperor Gratian and defeated him. The Emperor was then assassinated, and Maxen Wledig made himself the ruler of Britain, Gaul and Spain. He invaded Italy but was defeated and killed in 388.

The monastic movement, begun in the Egyptian desert, had spread to the south of France by the end of the fourth century. Maxen Wledig and his wife Helena, both Christians, fell under the influence of a Hungarian ex-soldier, known to the world ever since as Saint Martin of Tours. Martin had been Bishop of Tours since 372 but he was also a monk and essentially the founder of Celtic monasticism.

Until the time of Martin, the Christian Faith had been confined to urban centres, but he saw the possibilities of the monastery as a tool of evangelical outreach among the *pagani* (country folk) and exploited them to great effect. Tradition has it that, following the defeat and death of Maxen Wledig, his widow and her sons returned to her native Wales and established Martin's form of monasticism there.

Dr Kathleen Evans writes:

By the the beginning of the fifth century, monasticism was well established in Wales, as is attested by the very large number of place-names prefixed by *Llan*. The *llan* or *lanna* was originally an enclosure, and the term was later applied to the monastic buildings within it. A monastery was generally known by the name of its founder or head, as *Llanbadarn*, the *llan* or monastery of Padarn.

The monks would begin by digging a ditch and throwing up a great bank of earth around their land. Within this they would build small huts or cells, one for each of the monks with larger buildings for the church and refectory, and shelters for the animals. These huts would have double walls of wattles with the space between filled in with earth and stones. Later they would be replaced by stone buildings, beginning with the church.[2]

The Early Welsh Church

It was like a church to me.
I entered it on soft foot,
Breath held like a cap in the hand.

It was quiet.
What God was there made himself felt.
Not listened to, in clean colours
That brought a moistening of the eye.
In movement of the wind over grass.

R. S. Thomas[3]

The Welsh tribal culture into which the Christian Faith came was almost entirely rural. The four ancient dioceses of Saint David's, Saint Asaph's, Bangor and Llandaff each roughly covers the territory of one of the four main pre-Roman Celtic tribes.

Creation being the image of its Creator, the very land was holy and regarded as such, and not for nothing is the Welsh language regarded to this day as *iaith y nefoedd*, the language of heaven.

A monastery-based Church was the ideal solution to the problem of evangelism and ecclesiastical authority in a culture in which cities did not exist and territorial boundaries were always somewhat fluid. This caused the position of the bishop to differ somewhat from that of the Continental Church and was to cause controversy at a later date, and not only in Wales.

The head of the monastic community, like any of his monks, might or might not be in Holy Orders. Quite often he was a bishop – the great Welsh Churchman Dyfrig (d. 522) for instance, was head of a monastery and was in bishop's orders. Daughter communities came under the rule of the main community which then might be referred to as an 'archmonastery', and in that sense its episcopal head was an 'archbishop'. But the jurisdiction of a Welsh bishop was, for many centuries, congregational rather than territorial. It ideally suited the circumstances of the day and slowly changed into a territorial jurisdiction as the culture itself began to change.

Latin was the language of the early Welsh Church, and there is no evidence of the vernacular being used in the liturgy. The native language only came into very limited use much later when the language of the Roman Empire, like the Empire itself, became a dim folk-memory.

There was no significant liturgical difference between the Churches of Wales and Gaul, but it was not until 768 that the Roman date of Easter was adopted. The marriage of clergy not in monastic vows was normal and was the last of the differences in custom and discipline to be done away with.

It was not until the year 1188, nearly six hundred years after Augustine of Canterbury's ill-considered brush with the Celtic bishops, that the Welsh Church consented to come under the jurisdiction of Canterbury. And it was not until 1203 that the Diocese of Saint David's complied, its bishop, Giraldus Cambriensis, holding out almost to the very end.

The sixth and early seventh centuries were notable for the number of outstanding men and women produced by an evidently well-established and vigorous Welsh Church. The two earliest, and almost exact contemporaries, were Dyfrig (d.522), born in Herefordshire, and Illtud (d.525), who was probably a native of Brittany. Both men were bishops and heads of monasteries, Dyfrig finally of Ynys Enlli (Bardsey Island) and Illtud at Llantwit Major.

These two were the inspiration for a number of other great churchmen, among them David and Samson. David's father was Sant, King of Ceredigion (roughly modern Cardiganshire), and his mother, Non, is said to have been a nun. This suggests a style of Christian community which may not always have been celibate (but there is also a tradition concerning Non's seduction by King Sant). David himself, an energetic founder of communities, followed a strictly ascetic way of life, dying at his monastery in what is now Saint David's on the 1st of March 589.

Samson, Illtud's other great pupil, performed most of his later work first in Cornwall and then among the British immigrants in Brittany where he died at his monastery of Dol on the 28th of July 560.

There were many others, roughly contemporary. Cadog, who died a martyr's death in Brittany, had spent some time with the Church in Ireland, as had Cybi, the founder of the monastery at present-day Holyhead in Anglesey. Asaph (*d*.596) had been a pupil of the Brito-Pictish Saint Kentigern or Mungo (Munghu) whose own last years were spent in a community on the site of the present-day Glasgow Cathedral. Asaph was to give his name to Kentigern's foundation at Llanelwy, and the Cathedral of Saint Asaph's now stands on the spot.

THE ARTHURIAD

> And holy Dubric spread his hands and spake,
> 'Reign ye, and live and love, and make the world
> Other, and may the Queen be one with thee,
> And all this Order of the Table Round
> Fulfil the boundless purpose of their King!'
> Alfred Lord Tennyson, 'The Coming of Arthur'[4]

'Holy Dubric', in Tennyson's 'The Coming of Arthur', is none other than Dyfrig, whom the *Book of Llandaff* describes as 'Archbishop of Llandaff'. This he never was, nor did he ever crown Arthur as King. All this is heroically embroidered folk-memory, gathered into some kind of unity by Geoffrey of Monmouth (*d*.1154), Archdeacon of Saint Teilo's and later Bishop of Saint Asaph's.

Geoffrey's *Historia Britonum*, however doubtful as a work of history, is nevertheless something almost more important than a history. *It is a mythology!* It became a potent factor in the unification of England through its emphasis on the common origins of Britons, Saxons and Normans, and it proved to be an inspiration for chroniclers and poets.

It is to Wales that Britain owes, if not her soul, then certainly her fundamental archetypal images. And they are Celtic through and through. Logres, the archetypal Britain of the Arthurian Cycle, is identifiable with the western half of England, with Cornwall and with Wales, and with the Lowlands of Scotland up to the Clyde.

The Arthuriad, for so it can rightly be called, became not only the treasure-house of images and folk-tales for the great mass of the populace up until the Reformation, it was also to a considerable degree what might be described as a 'lay spirituality'. The Grail legends served to turn all normal values on their head and taught essentials of the Faith in vivid popular form, and with profound sacramental imagery.

In this, the Arthuriad bears comparison with the great Eastern popular religious mythologies, The *Ramayana* and the *Mahabaratha*. The 'Quest of the Holy Grail', in the Arthurian Cycle, corresponds remarkably in function to the 'Bhagavad Gita' in the Indian epic, the *Mahabaratha*.

NINIAN AND THE EARLY PICTISH CHURCH

Glen of the blue-eyed vigorous hawks,
glen abounding in every harvest,
glen of the ridged and pointed peaks,
glen of blackberries and sloes and apples.
Fourteenth-century Irish[5]

Saint Martin of Tours was to be influential not only in the evangelization of Wales, but he was also to profoundly influence the spread of the Christian

Faith north, across Hadrian's abandoned Wall and into that part of Scotland inhabited by the Britons and that most vigorous of peoples, the Picts.

In 394, a Cumbrian Christian by the name of Ninian (c. 360–432), who had been educated in Rome, was consecrated Bishop by Pope Siricius with a view to the conversion of Scotland to the Faith. On his journey north he came under the influence of Martin and determined upon a monastery-based approach to evangelism. He landed on the Isle of Whithorn in 397 and, with his companions, constructed the first stone-built church in Scotland.

From his secure base, Ninian, his companions and their successors, ranged all over southern Scotland, as far north as Sterling and Perth, and also into Fife and up the east coast a considerable distance – some would claim as far as Orkney and the Shetlands. According to A. B. Scott:

> While a native ministry was being reared, the ministry of the Church thus founded was sup-plied from the *muinntirs*, or religious com-munities of the Celtic Britons who lived south of the Wall of Antonine; and, also, from the reli-gious communities of the Irish Picts, particularly from the overflowing community of the Picts of Ulster at Bangor where St Comgall the Great ruled as Ab.[6]

Scott's reference to Irish Picts in Ulster no doubt concerns the P-Celtic minority who were still as yet unabsorbed by the Q-Celtic majority. The monastery at Bangor was sending missionaries to the Picts until at least the eighth century, as witness the mission of Maelrubba (d.722) who founded a monastery on the wild Applecross peninsula. From this holy wil-derness Maelrubba's mission evangelized the Isle of Skye and penetrated as far north as Loch Broom.

Scotland contained at least four distinct racial

groups at this period. Most numerous were the Picts, who were to be found throughout the land, but who were under pressure from Britons in the south-west (a Brito-Pictish Kingdom of Strathclyde, stretching from the Clyde to north Lancashire, survived until Norman times). Angles had invaded the south-east as far north as the Firth of Forth, and Q-Celtic-speaking Irish had established an extension to the Ulster Kingdom of Dalriada in Argyll and certain of the Isles.

The Pictish nation continued dominant until the Viking attacks in the ninth century, and their Church, like that of the Welsh was organized monastically with bishops-in-community holding a congregational rather than a territorial, jurisdiction.

To such a degree has romanticism lighted upon the Q-Celtic mission of Columba that the fact that the Pictish Church founded by Ninian flourished for *five hundred years* before it began to be merged with the Columban mission is almost universally forgotten.

The incursions of the Scotti, or Irish Q-Celtic speakers, into what we now call Scotland had already begun in the time of Ninian. Their progress east up the Great Glen was halted by the Pictish King Brude Mac Maelchon (d.584), whose capital was at Inverness. A very different Columban tradition from that usually accepted is cited by Scott when he claims:

> It was into the Pictish dominions thus defined, and to this sovereign, Brude Mac Maelchon, that, AD.563, SS Comgall and Cainnech, the Pictish ecclesiastical leaders, introduced St. Columba the Gaidheal, outcast from the Gaidheals of Ireland who had turned to the Dispersed among the Picts of Argyll.[7]

Brude is presented as a Christian king, and Columba a refugee, seeking a remote isle in the west from where he could minister to his own people on the west coast and in the Isles.

Scott is a splendidly partisan historian who accuses the later Columbans of re-writing history in their own favour and to the disparagement of Ninian and the Pictish Church.

COLUMBA'S (COLMCILLE'S) MISSION TO SCOTLAND

Woe to the Picts to whom he will go East,
He knew the thing that is,
It gave him no pleasure that a Gaidheal
Should reign in the East under the Picts.

Prophecy of Saint Berchan[8]

The fearsome, but yet immediately attractive figure of Columba (Colmcille) arrived on the isle of Iona in disputed circumstances in 563. According to his biographer Adomnan, he converted King Brude to the Faith, and in 574 consecrated an Irish King, Aidan, to the throne of Dalriada. Like Ninian he was believed to have converted vast areas single-handedly, but much of this is now believed to have been the work of his followers, or even of a near-namesake, Colm of Buchan.

The Columban mission certainly penetrated into Perthshire where a community was founded at Dull, and another at Dunkeld. In 842:

Kenneth Mac Alpin, king of the Gaidheals, or Scots of Dalriada, seated himself on the throne of the Picts in Fortrenn (Kingdom of Earn), and assumed the sovereignty. By this act, the King-ship of the Gaidhealic colony of Dalriada became merged in the High-kingship of Pictland.[9]

The foundations of Ninian and of Columba then merged, and the beginnings of a diocesan episcopacy can be traced with King Kenneth's appointment of Tuathal Mac Artguso as 'first bishop of Fortrenn (the entire Kingdom), Abbot of Duin Caillen [Dunkeld].'

Saint Andrews in Fife became the religious capital after Dunkeld (the cult of St Andrew was probably introduced into Scotland by the Northumbrian monks of Hexham), and Bishop Cellach of Saint Andrew's appeared on the Mote Hill of Scone with King Constantine III in AD 906. He seems to have been regarded as Bishop (or Chief Bishop) of all Scotland (Bishop of Alban).

The four peoples of Scotland gradually united. When Malcolm III Canmore ('bighead') married the Wessex princess Margaret in 1069, he took unto himself not only a much-loved wife but also an acknowledged saint. Through her influence and that of the later House of Canmore, the Scottish Church was established, for good or for ill, in the normal Continental Roman fashion. It was, alas, later destined to fall into a greater neglect and corruption than anywhere else in these islands, and the Reformation was to prove more extreme and more violent in Scotland than ever it was in England, Wales or Ireland.

It has been maintained that whereas St John was the inspiration of the Celtic Church, St Peter was that of the Roman. As J. D. Mackie comments:

'The Celtic Church gave love, the Roman Church gave law.' The epigram is as true as most epigrams, though doubtless both churches gave both.[10]

THE EVANGELIZATION OF IRELAND

I arise today
Through a mighty strength,
The invocation of the Trinity,
Through belief in the threeness,
Through confession of the oneness
Of the Creator of Creation.

Saint Patrick[11]

Patrick who, with his parents and grandfather in Cumbria, we have already met, was kidnapped by Irish raiders at the age of sixteen and taken into slavery, probably in what is now Mayo. After six years he escaped and eventually returned to his family, but found within himself a vocation to return to Ireland and begin the evangelization of that country.

He studied in Gaul, was ordained deacon in Auxerre, and sent to assist Palladius who was ministering to Irish Christians in Wicklow. On the death of Palladius, Patrick was consecrated Bishop by Germanus of Auxerre and proceeded to the court of the High King Laoghaire at Tara. In spite of determined opposition from the Druids, he gained toleration for the Faith and converted several of the royal household.

Patrick's was not the only mission to Ireland: many came from Britain and others from the Continent, among whom were Secundius, Auxilius, Declan and Tigernach. But Patrick's mission met with outstanding success, particularly in the northern half of the country. He died in 461, leaving a Church served by secular clergy under a local bishop, very much in the Continental style.

Ireland had no towns, however, and the Church soon adapted to the tribal organization of society and assigned to each bishop a diocese coterminous with the *tuath*, a commitment to an extended family grouping that carried a great emotional charge. The bishop had the same status as the king of the *tuath*.

Very soon the monastic life was established, as in other Celtic countries. The Irish social system laid great emphasis on kinship and personal rule, and readily welcomed the idea of the monastic 'family' under its abbot. Tribal monasteries were soon founded, and there was an astonishing flowering of literacy and learning. Irish scholars were soon to be found as far afield as Russia, and the 'holy Ireland' of the Druids was transformed into the 'holy Ireland' of the Christian monks.

It was a mere 102 years between the death of St Patrick and the departure of Colmcille (Columba) on his journey to Iona at the age of forty-two – so rapid and so profound had been Ireland's reception of the Faith. But why, and how? Frank Delaney, telling of his own boyhood, gives us an indication:

> At Mass on a Sunday morning in an Irish hillside church, the community took over. Though each individual worshipper was encouraged to contact God directly, all of us nonetheless belonged in communion – literally and figuratively. The mythology, whether Christian or pagan, or that vague and delicious brew of both, led us towards the stability created by belief.
>
> The system brought into play all the five senses ... Inculcation led towards communal harmony and moral coexistence. But at the basis, as the principal way and means, stood verbal communication. Narrative predominated: all the lessons taken from the higher authority, God or Jesus Christ, were transmitted as legend. Each and every Mass contained a Gospel ... The Celtic tales re-echoed. Christ the moral warrior ... the lines between his divinity and humanity never became clear.
>
> His childhood in the house at Nazareth received full display – as, in the Irish cycles, the childhood of Cuchulainn brought wondrous tales of silver hurley and golden ball ... Lugh of the Long Arm could leap on a bubble without bursting it: Christ walked on water ... the Christian Gospels were preceded in the Irish consciousness by legends such as the Fenian cycles – the stories of Finn McCool.[12]

That vague and delicious brew of both, led us into the

stability created by belief. Christ was seen, not only as the meaning and fulfilment of history, but – almost more importantly – as the meaning and fulfilment of mythology. The Druids were not destroyed, they and their tradition were redeemed, transfigured, fulfilled. The *whole person* was addressed, the rational being and the intuitive being. And there being no taint of the Augustinian perversion of the Faith into world-rejection, its reception was as immediate as it was remarkable.

COLMCILLE'S EXILE

He was born at Gartan by his consent;
And he was nursed at Cill-nic-Neoin;
And the son of goodness was baptised,
At Tulach Dubhglaise of God.

Saint Mura[13]

On the 7th of December 521 Colmcille was born at Gartan in Donegal. His father, Fedhlimidh, was descended from Conal Gulban and so he was a prince of the Northern Ui Neill. His mother, by later tradition, was descended from the kings of Leinster, and so Colmcille's social rank was on a par with that of the High King.

Colmcille became a monk and, with spiritual zeal combined with social standing, he was a great founder of monasteries. The first was at Doire Cholmcille (Derry) and others followed. Colmcille was in fact building up a *paruchia* (or 'parish') of tribal monasteries, and while thus engaged one of the Southern Ui Neill, Diarmid, was building up his own secular power-base until, in 558, he felt powerful enough to proclaim himself High King at Tara, using the ancient pagan rites for the purpose.

The Christianization of Ireland was too recent, and

paganism still too powerful, for this to go unchallenged. Colmcille became involved in the mustering of the forces of the Northern Ui Neill, and the clash took place at the decisive battle of Cul Dreibne, near one of Colmcille's monasteries (Droim Chliabh) at the foot of Ben Bulben. Diarmid suffered a crushing defeat.

By the standards of the time it was a bloody carnage with some three thousand dead. Colmcille's involvement in the politics that led up to the battle was probably the reason for his exile – imposed or self-imposed – to Scotland, in order to save as many souls for Christ as fell in the battle.

For whatever reason, Colmcille became the archetype for the *peregrini Christi* – wanderers for Christ – the Irish missionaries who were to bring the Gospel to parts of Continental Europe over the next few centuries.

6·THE CENTURIES OF SORROWS

Here there were priests and bells,
hymns, and theology being read,
choral song and music
praising the majesty of God.

Useless and empty ruin,
dwelling-place with your ancient towers,
many a storm and wind
has lashed the bare tops of your walls.
                              Sean O. Coileain[1]

Almost exactly two hundred years after the death of Colmcille (Columba), the Vikings raided the Columban foundation of Lindisfarne and burned its monastery to the ground. The following year it was the turn of Monkwearmouth to go up in flames, then Iona itself. From 794 until 836 the whole of the coastal areas of Scotland and northern England lived in an agony of terror. Nobody was safe and nothing was sacred.

After a brief respite, due to political turbulence in Norway, Harald Haarfagre siezed power and a determined Viking expansion began into Scotland, northern England and Ireland. The Scots kingdom of Dalriada was overrun, the Isles passed into Viking hands (the last was to be returned to Scotland in 1462), and one by one the Irish monasteries went up in flames.

With the passage of time Norse and Gael settled down to an uneasy peace. In Ireland, however, the Norse power was broken in 1014 by the High King Brian Boraimhe at a decisive battle near Dublin. At the end of the century an attempt was made by the warrior king Magnus Berfott to re-establish Norse power but he was ambushed, overwhelmed and slain in 1103. Ireland was to enjoy two-and-a-half centuries of peace until the next onslaught upon her.

During the ninth century, the Vikings broke the power of the Picts in Scotland and possibly thus hastened the merging of the four nations of Scotland into one. In the west, the Viking Kingdom of Man controlled all the western Isles and some of the mainland coastal areas. In the twelfth century, a dispute arose between Godred, King of Man, and his brother-in-law, Somerled. A naval battle in the Sound of Jura settled the matter, and the two divided the Isles between them, Somerled taking all the Isles south of Ardnamurchan except the Isle of Man itself. Somerled was thus the first Lord of the Isles, an independent, Celtic, island state for four hundred years.

It is interesting to note that Somerled, whose name establishes him as Viking, was 'whitewashed' by his bards and declared to have been the son of one Gille-Bhride, a supposed Celtic bane of all Norsemen! Be that as it may, two leading Scottish families, the MacDonalds and the MacDougals, very properly claim descent from Somerled.

Viking power in and around Scotland was finally broken at the Battle of Largs in 1263 by which time Norse and Gael had substantially merged into the one heroic tribal culture which was to survive in the Highlands and Islands until 1745.

In England, Viking and Dane gradually took control of the eastern half of the country, thus repeating the earlier conquest pattern of the Anglo-Saxons. By the end of the tenth century there was a considerable merging of cultures, and by the time of the Norman Conquest England was, to all intents and purposes, a single Christian nation with Celtic, Anglo-Saxon and Danish blood mingling by intermarriages. The British Celt on the English side of the Welsh border was by this time fast losing any separate identity.

THE COMING OF THE NORMANS

The hall of Cynddylan,
it pierces me to see it without roof,
without fire;
my lord dead, myself alive . . .

The chapels of Bassa have lost their rank
after the destruction by the English
of Cynddylan and Elfan of Powys . . .
Ninth-century Welsh[2]

The coming to England of William the Conqueror in 1066 brought a far more serious threat to the embattled Celts than any they had faced hitherto. The Normans, themselves descended from Viking invaders of France of an earlier generation, brought with them not only an insatiable lust for power and conquest but also a political system utterly alien, not only to the Celts but no less to the Anglo-Saxon. The feudal system replaced the strong ties of an extended family (the Irish *tuath*) with serfdom under a foreign tyrant in his stone-built castle.

The feudal system soon enslaved the native English, and the Norman kings began to look further afield.

King Henry II (1154—89) prevailed upon the only Englishman ever to occupy the papal throne, Hadrian IV, to grant him the overlordship of Ireland, Ireland being 'irreligious' and thus in need of Christian conquest – and the payment of more regular financial tribute to Rome!

The papal bull which granted this honour, *Laudabiliter*, is now generally recognized to have been a forgery but, armed with such impeccable credentials, Henry II was quick to respond to an opportunity which arose almost twenty years later. A disgruntled king, Dermot MacMurrough of Leinster, sought assistance from Henry in seizing national power from his rivals. He might as well have asked the devil for assistance against sin!

Two invasions, a year apart, established a precarious Norman English lordship over Ireland, and the Synod of the Irish Church at Cashel in 1171 abolished the Celtic system of monastic – even tribal – episcopacy in favour of the Continental system of bishops with territorial jurisdictions.

The Synod of Cashel went further. It abolished Gaelic liturgies, re-established Latin as the liturgical language (where it had lapsed), and decreed that all services 'shall be celebrated according to the usage of the Church of England'.

Wales fought the Normans and their successors, off and on, for three hundred years. Paradoxically, it was a mostly Welsh infantry (chiefly their archers) who won the battles of Crecy, Poitiers and Agincourt for the English in their Hundred Years War against the French.

Scotland suffered from a determined attempt at conquest by Edward I (1272–1307) but won her freedom (though not by any means her peace) at the Battle of Bannockburn in 1314. She was a divided nation and would remain so until after 1745. The King's writ ran south of the Highland line; beyond lay the old heroic tribal culture of the

Clans and their allegiance to the Scottish Crown was decidedly conditional. The Gaelic language was spoken throughout in the countryside, although Scots (Scots English) was latterly the language of officialdom.

THE CENTRAL CHARACTERISTICS OF CELTIC CHRISTIANITY

*Bless to me, O God, the moon that is above
me,
Bless to me, O God, the earth that is beneath
me,
Bless to me, O God, my wife and my children,
And bless, O God, myself who have care of
them;
Bless to me my wife and my children,
And bless, O God, myself who have care of
them.*

Carmina Gadelica[3]

The political assaults upon the Celtic peoples, their culture and their integrity were one thing, their Christian Faith was quite another. As always, it flowered in adversity.

The characteristics of the Christian Faith of the Celts were not peculiar to them, either then or now. They are in fact the essential wholeness of the Christian vision. They can be stated thus:

1. An intense awareness that the world – indeed the whole Universe – is the transfigured image of God, charged at every point with His Glory.

*[Christ] loved the earth, loved it as a lover
because it is God's earth;*

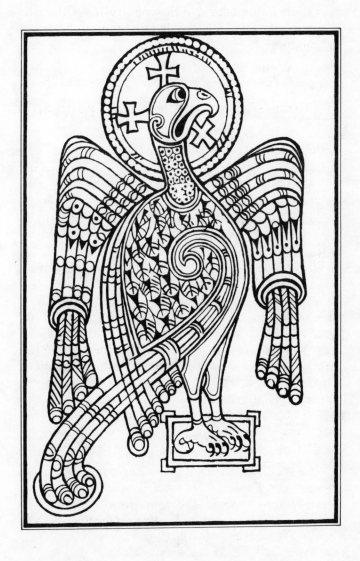

Eagle of St. John with halo and crosses, Gospel of St. Matthew. Book of Kells.

> He loved it, because it was created by His
> Father from nothingness to be Life's temple.
>
> Donald Evans[4]

2. A vivid awareness of the Risen Christ, glorious and beautiful, and yet humiliated still in the sufferings of the poor. There is no sense of 'Gentle Jesus meek and mild', no sentimentality, but there is a great – and mutual – tenderness.

3. A clear vision of the whole Church (the *organism* rather than the organization) as immersed in and radiant with 'the Oneness of the Trinity'.

Saint John (beloved of the Celt) tells us that 'God is Love'. This is, perhaps, the Christian revelation in a nutshell. The realization that *God is also a Love-Affair* sums up the Doctrine of the Trinity in a nutshell, and about this there is no confusion in any of the Celtic writings or prayers.

God is One and indivisible, but within the unity there is – blessedly but unimaginably – a Trinity. *This is the Christian experience of God.* And Christians are caught up in the Love-Affair which is God. This is why Christ came, why 'the Word became flesh and dwelt among us'.

> The Three who are over my head,
> The Three who are under my tread,
> The Three who are over me here,
> The Three who are over me there,
> The Three who are in the earth near,
> The Three who are up in the air.
> The Three who in heaven do dwell,
> The Three in the great ocean swell,
> Pervading Three, O be with me![5]

4. Above all else there is a passionate knowledge of

the unutterable tenderness and mercy of God, the truth beyond every other truth.

> *I see this one today coming towards me*
> *across Tir Coch,*
> *beckoning with the hands*
> *that are warm with his own blood.*
> *I hear him call too*
> *in the accents of Nant Conwy.*
>
> Meirion Evans[6]

THE COMING OF THE REFORMATION

> *The compassing of God be on thee,*
> *The compassing of the God of life.*
>
> *The compassing of Christ be on thee,*
> *The compassing of the Christ of love.*
>
> *The compassing of Spirit be on thee,*
> *The compassing of the Spirit of Grace.*
>
> *The compassing of the Three be on thee,*
> *The compassing of the Three preserve thee.*
> *The compassing of the Three preserve thee.*
>
> Carmina Gadelica[7]

The first fourteen hundred years of the Christian Faith among the Celtic peoples saw their fair share of battle, murder and sudden death. Gradually, the remaining paganism among their brother Celts was assimilated and fulfilled, and gradually those invaders who had settled among them were also brought into the one fold.

The Normans who remained in Ireland, mostly in the Pale around Dublin, were rapidly becoming 'more Irish than the Irish'. This was in spite of such monstrosities as the Statutes of Kilkenny (1366) which forbade intermarriage, or even the admission of Irish musicians and storytellers to English households. An English subject heard speaking Irish was liable to have his lands confiscated. This was indicative of an English official state of mind which was to persist for another six hundred years.

By the time of the Reformation, Ireland, Wales and Scotland (particularly north of the Highland line) were the main strongholds of the Celts. The old heroic tribal culture was still strong, and the common Christian Faith, though officially subordinate to Rome, was remote enough from the Continent to remain essentially indigenous.

In England it would probably be true to say that the character of the Church altered little until the coming of the Normans. Thereafter it suited the kings of England to keep the papacy at arm's length. Celtic Christianity differed from English only insomuch as the Celt differs from the Englishman, and lest this be overstated it is good to remember that there remains not a little Celtic blood in English veins to this very day.

The Renaissance and, hard on its heels, the Reformation constituted a profound assault upon the very soul of the Celtic people. One besetting weakness of the Celt is his tendency towards internecine strife, another is his determination to see everything in terms of black or white, and neither to forget nor ever quite forgive. The Reformation in Scotland, where the Church had fallen into great corruption and decay, was thus a harrowing, bitter and often brutal business. Calvinism was to become the religion of Scotland and to claim the allegiance of most of its people.

In England, reforming zeal joined forces both with rapacious royal greed and with the utmost administrative cynicism. The English Church, plundered and severed from Rome but only moderately reformed, retained the allegiance of the great mass of the people, as did also the Church in Wales.

In Ireland, the Reformation became a tool in the hands, first of the Tudors, then of the Stuarts, Cromwell and finally William of Orange. A fresh and sustained attempt was made over two whole centuries to conquer the country once and for all. The tribal culture was pinned down and finally destroyed by the settlement of an imported population, first of northern English, and later of southern Scots.

The imported population were of the Church of England, and the Church of Ireland was established almost entirely among the English in Ireland. The Scottish settlers brought Calvinism with them, and religious strife soon became a three-way battle, for the great Celtic mass of the population clung steadfastly to the Church of their fathers. However, Anglican and Calvinist were at one politically, for all religious freedom and access to education were to be denied to Catholics until the very end of the eighteenth century.

The Celts in general, and the Irish in particular, were thereafter to enjoy virtual sub-human status, and every effort was to be made at least until the time of Queen Victoria to destroy their culture, their languages and their identity.

THE EFFECTS OF THE REFORMATION

The eye of the great God,
The eye of the God of glory,
The eye of the King of hosts,
The eye of the King of the living,
Pouring upon us
At each time and season,
Pouring upon us
Gently and generously.

> *Glory to thee,*
> *Thou glorious sun.*
>
> *Glory to thee, the sun,*
> *Face of the God of life.*
> Carmina Gadelica[8]

In an earlier chapter we touched upon the distorting pessimism of Saint Augustine of Hippo, his obsession with original sin, and an original guilt which he believed accompanied it. Sex he firmly and specifically identified with sin; and world-rejection, a doctrine of arbitrary predestination of some souls for heaven and the eternal condemnation of the rest, troubled the mind of this otherwise great, good and saintly man. It also gained a certain currency in a Western Church always slightly predisposed to receive it. While never the official teaching of the Church, it was nevertheless respectable. Echoes of it were often heard, and international calamities such as the Black Death tended to bring such morbid but questionably Biblical speculations back into mind.

The Renaissance brought with it a rediscovery of Holy Scripture, and the invention of the printing press made it widely available. The Old Testament became a source of great – if uncritical – inspiration, and 'theocracies' were set up by many of the early reformers, the most formidable of whom was John Calvin.

Calvin was an extreme Augustinian. Mankind was 'totally depraved' by the Fall of Adam. All Augustine's darkest thoughts were to be found darker still in the mind of Calvin. Martin Luther was also an Augustinian, both in thought and in upbringing, for he had been a member of the Augustinian Order. The mind of Saint Augustine of Hippo inspired many of the doctrines of all the great reformers. It has to be said for them that their driving concern was for godliness in a Church sunk in what must have seemed to them to be an irredeemable mess of corruption, power-seeking, money-grubbing and worldliness. It is perhaps small wonder that the vivid images of the wrathful God of the Old Testament and the intellectual gloom of Saint Augustine worked so mightily upon them.

So utterly alien was all this to the Celtic Christian experience that the Reformation trauma must have been extreme.

The Reformation was to a considerable degree a revolt by intellectuals. The focus of religion was effectively shifted from the heart to the head. In Scotland, popular education became a religious crusade, for the people must be enabled to read their Bibles and think for themselves. Not only was the intellectual climate essentially non-mystical, it speedily became positively anti-mystical. The intuition was suspect – it became regarded as the realm of the devil and his angels. In Scotland alone, over the course of two-and-a-half centuries, between four and five thousand people were to be burned alive for a 'witchcraft' which was as often as not little more than the possession and use of a higher than usual degree of intuitive perception.

The consequences of the Reformation trauma, together with the political use of religious controversy – not to mention the importation into Ireland of a population alien in both race and understanding of their common Christian Faith – are with us to this day. They constitute the 'shadow side' of Celtic Christianity which it would be as unrealistic to ignore as it would be dishonest.

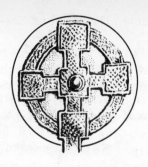

7·CELTIC? CATHOLIC? OR SIMPLY ORTHODOX?

. . . What shall we do
with the pansy Christ
who hangs high
on the walls of the memory's vestries?

We shall tear
the petticoat that is about him
so that we see the eternal arms
all hair and muscles
and the hands like shovels
whipping synods and government.

Meirion Evans[1]

But for the Reformation, nobody would be talking or speculating about 'Celtic Christianity'.

Such has been the conditioning of the past four-and-a-half centuries that, true or false, it is extremely difficult to avoid a sectarian interpretation of this remark. Nevertheless the attempt must be made, for that cataclysmic upheaval of the Western Church which goes by the name of the Reformation was the consequence of two main factors.

First was the sink of worldliness, corruption, and latterly, fiendish cruelty into which the papacy had fallen ever more deeply since Hildebrand (Pope Gregory VII, d.1085). By the early fourteenth century, merely to think for oneself was to risk being burned alive. Second was the Renaissance of learning, the rediscovery of the classics and the invention of the printing press. Set this in a Western Europe deeply traumatized by the Black Death and the threat of Turkish conquest, and all the spiritual, psychological and intellectual ingredients were assembled for explosive rebellion against a thoroughly discredited *status quo*. The explosion, when it came, was cataclysmic and destructive in a sense which is only now being fully appreciated.

In the midst of this turmoil, and probably as a result of it, the morbid theological speculations of Saint Augustine of Hippo flowered at their darkest in the mind of John Calvin, and only slightly less darkly in the minds of most of the other reformers. This we have noted in the last chapter. But Augustine was to find a new incarnation in the mind of Cornelius Otto Jansen (d. 1638), and 'Jansenism', though officially condemned by Rome, gained entry through a series of 'back doors' and has imparted a somewhat Augustinian cast of mind to a great deal of the post-Reformation Roman Catholic Church ever since.

In brief, 'Jansenism' maintained that without a special gift of grace from God, the performance of His commandments is impossible for men and women. Furthermore, the operation of God's grace is irresistible, and thus mankind is the victim of either a natural or a supernatural determinism. This theological pessimism was expressed in a general harshness and moral rigorism. Indeed a rigorist tendency in all matters of ecclesiastical discipline has characterized this movement from the first, as has a violent antagonism to liberalism in any shape or form and particularly as manifested in the Society of Jesus, better known as the Jesuits.

The Roman Catholic Church in Ireland, at least since its emancipation at the end of the eighteenth century, has manifested a decidedly 'Jansenist' cast of mind. The dolours of Saint Augustine's psycho-sexual problems and their rationalization in theological pessimism have thus been visited upon the Celtic Christian from both ecclesiastical directions in recent centuries. It is a matter of blessed astonishment that to a very large degree he has succeeded in transcending them.

REASONS FOR A CELTIC REVIVAL

More bitter to me than Death coming between my teeth are the folk that will come after me . . .

The Elders who did God's will at the beginning of time were bare-haunched, scurvy, muddy: they were not stout and fat!

The men of keen learning, who served the King of the Sun, did not molest boys or women; their natures were pure.

Scanty shirts, clumsy cloaks, hearts weary and piteous, short rough shocks of hair – and very rough monastic rules.

There will come after that the Elders of the latter-day world, with plunder, with cattle, with mitres, with rings, with chessboards . . .

I tell the seed of Adam, the hypocrites will

come, they will assume the shape of God – the
slippery ones, the robbers!

Twelfth-century Irish[2]

The Irishman who wrote of 'The Elders of the End of
the World' lived at the time of the English invasion
and the Synod of Cashel in 1171 at which the traditional Irish monastic episcopate was abolished in
favour of Continental-style episcopacy. With a wry
black humour, he saw all the possibilities of future
corruption, even then beginning to be manifested
throughout the Western Church.

The revived interest in 'Celtic Christianity' springs
in part from an awareness that the Church has become
too much identified with worldly power-structures,
all claiming divine authority. This is the case (though
differently manifested) on both sides of the Reformation divide. In addition, there is an awareness that
the Gospel has become altogether too academicized
and that the resulting primacy of intellect threatens
not only equilibrium but wholeness as well.

The mainspring of the 'Celtic Revival' in this
respect, however, is an urgent desire – however
articulated – to recover a Christian Faith that is big
enough to embrace the totality of life's experience.
Nothing less will do. Anything else is a distortion, a
compromise, a counterfeit.

There is an awakening to the realization that, not
only is the whole 'pessimism package' associated
with Saint Augustine Biblically questionable and
evidently subjective, but that in terms of the life,
character and teachings of Christ it is positively
pathological.

It is also attractive to – and has attracted – both
the ecclesiastical rigorist and disciplinarian upon the
one hand, and the Puritan and the 'hell-fire preacher'
on the other. And for very similar – though usually
unconscious – reasons.

The temptation to romanticize about the Celtic

Church must, however, be resisted. And it is as well to be reminded that 'The Elders who did God's will at the beginning of time' were 'men of keen learning . . . their natures were pure . . . hearts weary and piteous . . . and very rough monastic rules!' There is nothing cosy or romantic about the authentic Christian Revelation. Everlasting Love is totally demanding, even to death. Anything else is a sentimental counterfeit.

THE CONTEMPLATIVE LIFE

Alone in my little hut without a human being
in my company,
dear has been the pilgrimage before going
to meet death.

A remote hidden little cabin,
for forgiveness of my sins;
a conscience upright and spotless
before holy Heaven . . .

Eighth-century Irish[3]

The Celtic Church depended upon its monastic communities, and those communities reflected the prevailing culture in that they were tribal both in character and in composition. Colmcille set sail for Scotland and Iona with companions who were his own kinsmen in that they were his fellow-tribesmen. But the monastery was the centre of all evangelistic outreach. The whole life and work of the Celtic Church depended upon lives lived in contemplative prayer. All its activity proceeded from contemplation.

In such circumstances the 'mystical' is normal. As Catherine Docherty puts it:

There is a difference between what the East means by mystical and what the West means. I think the East would call normal many things that the West might think mystical. If you are in the 'desert' and God knocks on your door and speaks to you, that doesn't sound mystical to me; it sounds quite normal. He said he would speak to us!

Catherine Docherty, despite her Irish name, is Russian, and was brought up within the whole ambience of Russian spirituality. The Orthodox Churches of the Christian East have not only been 'discovered' by Western Christians in recent years, but have also begun to exert an influence altogether out of proportion to their numerical size in Western countries. And many who have looked longingly towards the Celtic past have been astonished to discover what they are looking for in contemporary Orthodoxy.

In an earlier chapter, I mentioned my Polish friend who had discovered, during the war, an unexpected possibility of communication between Gaelic-speaking Scots and Polish-speaking Poles. A warning was given against over-romantic speculation as to how and why. A not dissimilar warning must be given concerning apparent similarities between contemporary Orthodoxy and what we imagine the Celtic Church to have been like.

Nevertheless some likenesses may cautiously be discerned, for Eastern spirituality is in some important respects different from Western and — just possibly — closer to the Celtic. To begin with, the writ of Saint Augustine of Hippo has never run in the Eastern Church.

The Christian East knows no 'Monastic Orders', each with its own style, its own rule, its own traditions, its own power-structures and its tendency to compete with other Orders in ways, sometimes trivial, sometimes not. There are no Benedictines, Franciscans, Dominicans, Augustinians, Carmelites, and all the very many other Orders of both men and women. There are simply those in Monastic

Vows (there are a number of degrees of solemnity in vows), and those in Monastic Vows usually live in monasteries. The commitment to a contemplative life in celibacy is what constitutes a monk or a nun, not the joining of a specific Monastic Order with its inevitably complicating loyalties to the Order itself.

In the Christian East, as once in the Celtic West, there is a tradition of retreat into the 'desert' (Russian: *poustinia*), to a solitary hermitage, for a specified period or sometimes for the rest of this life. Most of Catherine Docherty's description of *poustinia* and the *poustinikki* relates sufficiently to what we can find in descriptions of Celtic hermits and hermitages to be worth attending to in our present study:

> Usually the poustinik was a man, though there were women poustinikki also. Sometimes they were single people, sometimes they were widows and widowers. Not all of them were educated in the academic sense of the word . . . Whoever these people were, they were not necessarily old in age . . . Usually they were people who went into the poustinia around the age of thirty or thirty-five. Others may have been older, in their late fifties or early sixties who had been married, reared their children, and then felt the attraction of the desert.
>
> There was no big fuss about going into a poustinia. From some village, from some noble-man's house, from some merchant's house – from any part of our society in Russia – a man would arise. (Of course, only God knows *why* he did arise.) He would arise and go into the place (as the Russians say) 'where heaven meets earth,' departing without any earthly goods, usu-ally dressed in the normal dress of a pilgrim . . . to pray to God for [his] sins and the sins of the world, to atone, to fast, to live in poverty, and to enter the great silence of God.
>
> There were other poustinikki, both men and

women, who had been monks and nuns . . .
these people would get permission from their
abbots or abbesses to become poustinikki, dwell-
ers of the poustinia and the desert.[4]

This contemporary description of Russia as Catherine
remembered it from her childhood and from her
knowledge of its traditions, relates strongly to such
Celtic 'deserts' as we know of from study, and occasionally encounter in life. There is a timelessness
about some of them which quite transcends the centuries. (Catherine Docherty's descriptions ring true to
me on more than one level – one of them being, quite
simply, that of *encounter*.)

There is a tendency to dwell too much upon the
sheer asceticism involved, and an 'Augustinian' cast
of mind can quite easily slip into putting a value on
asceticism for asceticism's own sake. This is always
an error. The rigours of early Celtic Christian life in
any circumstances would seem ascetic beyond reason
to the present-day comfortable suburb-dweller! The
asceticism of the Celtic hermit – as of his brother
the Russian poustinik – is better understood as the
embracing of an absolute simplicity.

Scanty shirts, clumsy cloaks, hearts weary and
piteous, short rough shocks of hair – and very
rough monastic rules.[5]

Catherine Docherty, in the book quoted, was concerned to promote 'the desert' as a vital part of the
life of the busy, distracted Western Christian. We
should all, in some way or another, have our own
poustinia and enter its peace from time to time. This
is the theme of her book. Once there:

. . . since the reason for entering the poustinia is
one of listening to God in prayer and fasting, the
first act of a poustinik is *to fold the wings of his*

intellect and open the doors of his heart. The Russians would say: Put your head into your heart and try to achieve a deep and profound silence. It is then, when one is deeply silent, that God begins to speak.[6]

CREATOR AND CREATION AS ONE

My Creator to visit me, my Lord, my King,
my spirit to seek Him in the eternal kingdom
where He is.

Eighth-century Irish[7]

As we have discovered, the influence of Saint Augustine of Hippo has impinged upon the Celtic Christian from both ecclesiastical directions during the centuries since the Reformation. The reformed tradition has been intellectualist and non-mystical – even anti-mystical. The intuition has been suspect, even identified with darkness.

The Catholic tradition has been more fortunate. Even the Jansenist cast of mind, with all its rigorism, cannot deny or escape from the profound tradition of Christian mysticism which the Western Church has always lovingly nurtured and rightly venerated. Anyone who reads the great Christian mystics will find all the sensitivities of the intuition very much present, set in the context of deep prayer and seen in a proper perspective.

Within the embrace of the life and experience of the total Church, the various perceptive gifts of the Faithful and that whole realm known as the 'psychic' find their proper context and also the way to their fulfilment. The Faith does indeed embrace the totality of life's experience – as indeed it must – but the commandment is ever to seek *first* the Kingdom of God and His righteousness, and then all the rest will follow.

The Faith must also not only embrace, but be totally identified with, the whole of human life and the living of it. It is here that the Christianity of the Celt has triumphed over the limiting influences of post-Reformation ecclesiasticism of all kinds. There is a cost, however, and it must occasionally manifest in a schizoid separation of 'kirk religion' from the religion of the heart and of the hearth.

This latter is well exemplified by a remark made by a Lochaber woman to her grandchildren, recorded by Alexander Carmichael in his *Carmina Gadelica*: 'Be still, children, be quiet, you would cause the mild Mary of grace to sin!' The good woman was devoutly and sternly Protestant, and her easy familiarity with the Mother of God, common among the Gaels and belonging to her Celtic Christian inheritance, would have no place in the kirk she devoutly attended every Sunday.

Essentially the Celt is devout rather than religious. There being none of the unreal separation of religion from life in his inheritance, there is nothing to be 'religious' about. Devotion – love – is his natural response to a total unity of experience of the loving Creator and the Creation which is the transfigured image of its Creator. It comes easily to the Celt to 'put his head in his heart'.

When the Celt becomes 'religious' and manifests pious religiosity rather than devotion, then something is seriously – and often horribly – amiss.

THE INTERWEAVING OF PAGAN LEGEND AND GOSPEL TRUTH

> *Go shorn and come woolly,*
> *Bear the Beltane female lamb,*
> *Be the lovely Bride thee endowing,*
> *And the fair Mary thee sustaining,*
> *The fair Mary sustaining thee.*
> *Carmina Gadelica*[8]

In the 1526 edition of the English Sarum Missal, the summer and winter solstices, the spring and autumn equinoxes, and the passage of the sun through the zodiac, rubbed shoulders with the feasts and fasts of Holy Church.

Tactfully, the Church had 'baptized' the old pagan feasts. *Oimelc* was celebrated as the Feast of Saint Bride (who herself assimilated the pagan goddess of her name). *Beltane* became the feast of Saint Philip and Saint James, *Lughsnadh* the feast of Saint Peter's Chains or Lammas (loaf-mass, the first-fruits of harvest), and *Samhain* the feast of All Hallows.

The winter solstice on the 21st of December was now the Feast of Saint Thomas; the summer solstice on the 21st of June (belatedly on the 24th) became the Nativity of Saint John the Baptist; the spring equinox (the 21st of March) was belatedly Lady Day on the 25th; and the autumn equinox was the feast of Saint Matthew. In 1526 the slippage caused by the Julian Calendar then in use showed the solstice and equinox dates as the 14th of December, 11th of March, 13th of June and 14th of September, thus giving the Church's original game away!

Our Lord, as He said, 'came not to destroy but to fulfil,' and all that was best and true in paganism was embraced and fulfilled. This is beautifully expressed in *The Beltane Blessing*:

Bless, O Threefold true and bountiful,
Myself, my spouse, and my children,
My tender children and their beloved mother
at their head.
On the fragrant plain, on the gay mountain
sheiling,
On the fragrant plain, on the gay mountain
sheiling.

Everything within my dwelling or in my
possession,

> *All kine and crops, all flocks and corn,*
> *From Hallow Eve to Beltane Eve,*
> *With goodly progress and gentle blessing,*
> *From sea to sea, and every river mouth,*
> *From wave to wave, and base of waterfall . . .*
> *Carmina Gadelica*[9]

A feature of Celtic Christianity has always been the consecration of the landscape by the performance of 'stations'. The setting up of great stone crosses and the consecration of ancient standing stones with the cross has from the first been a feature of the Faith among the Celts. It continues the ancient wisdom out of its 'old testament' into its new.

The visiting of such places – crosses, wells, prominent or significant points of the landscape – and perambulating them three times clockwise reciting the *Credo*, the *Pater Noster* and the *Ave Maria*, still goes on and fulfils a deep need in the Celtic soul. Prayer *done* rather than merely *said* is deeply satisfying and has always been the spur to pilgrimages of all kinds.

There is another side to this, however. Activity of this sort is part of the fulfilment of the 'priesthood of man', Christian man in particular. Mankind is priest to the whole of the natural order, articulating its praise to its Creator and representing both God to Creation and Creation to God. This is why the performance of 'stations' is so curiously satisfying.

Heaven and earth are at one in the hearts of the Faithful – the saints, the holy angels, the well, and the man and woman at the well, are bound together in a bond of love:

> *The shelter of Mary Mother*
> *Be nigh my hand and feet*
> *To go out to the well*
> *And to bring me safely home.*
> *And to bring me safely home.*

> *May warrior Michael aid me,*
> *May Brigit calm preserve me,*
> *May sweet Brianag give me light,*
> *And Mary pure be near me,*
> *And Mary pure be near me.*
>
> Carmina Gadelica[10]

With Catholic emancipation in Ireland, a tremendous programme of church-building was undertaken. There was a consequent movement of the Sunday Mass from 'stations' in farm buildings, at open-air 'mass-rocks' and such-like expedients of persecution, and a consequent 'ecclesiasticizing' of Irish devotional life, as R. F. Foster reports:

> From the 1850s religious societies proliferated; devotional aids and new devotions became the norm: the rosary, forty hours, perpetual adoration, novenas, blessed altars, *Via Crucis*, benediction, vespers, devotion to the Sacred Heart and to the Immaculate Conception, jubilees, triduums, pilgrimages, shrines, processions and retreats.
>
> These tended to replace holy wells, bonfires, 'patterns', wakes, protective charms, effigies and the ancient celebration of high points in the agricultural calendar. Contemporaries noticed the abandonment of magical practices in rural life from the late 1840s.

One is tempted to wonder if as much was lost as was gained in this shift of devotional emphasis!

Pagan legend and Gospel truth are interwoven in Celtic devotion – and rightly so, for Christ is the meaning and fulfilment of all mythology, just as He is Lord of history. A rationalist mind, accustomed to living in prose and inclined to be dismissive of poetry, would find the *Genealogy of Bride* superstitious – even dangerous! I readily confess that I find it delightful!

The genealogy of the holy maiden Bride,
Radiant flame of gold, foster-mother of Christ.
Bride the daughter of Dugall the brown,
Son of Aidh, son of Art, son of Conn,
Son of Crearar, son of Cis, son of Carmac, son
of Carruin.

Every day and every night
That I say the genealogy of Bride,
I shall not be killed, I shall not be harried,
I shall not be put in cell, I shall not be wounded,
Neither shall Christ leave me in forgetfulness.

No fire, no sun, no moon shall burn me,
No lake, no water, nor sea shall drown me,
No arrow of fairy nor dart of fay shall wound me,
And I under the protection of my Holy Mary,
And my gentle foster-mother is my beloved
Bride.

Carmina Gadelica[11]

No less delightful is the *Charm of the Yarrow*. My hope is that all the Highland girls who breathed their girlish hopes over the smooth yarrow had their wishes fulfilled:

I will pick the smooth yarrow that my figure may be more elegant, that my lips may be warmer, that my voice may be more cheerful; may my voice be like a sunbeam, may my lips be like the juice of the strawberries.

May I be an island in the sea, may I be a hill on the land, may I be a star when the moon wanes, may I be a staff to the weak one: I shall wound every man, no man shall wound me![12]

8·CELTIC CHRISTIANITY – SO WHAT?

Thou King of moon and sun,
Thou King of stars beloved,
Thou Thyself knowest our need,
O Thou merciful God of life.
          Carmina Gadelica[1]

In his book, *Celtic Britain*, Charles Thomas says, of Celtic Britain and Ireland:

> ... those popular phrases 'the Celtic Church' and 'Celtic Christianity' must, in view of the universality of Christianity, be deplored as both misleading and inaccurate.[2]

In the introductory essay to *A Celtic Miscellany*, K. H. Jackson maintains that:

> ... since the time when Macpherson exploited Celtic sources to provide a public eager for Romantic material with what they wanted, it has been the fashion to think of the Celtic mind as something mysterious, magical, filled

with dark broodings over a mighty past; and the Irish, Welsh, and the rest as a people who by right of birth alone were in some strange way in direct contact with a mystical supernatural twilight world which they would rarely reveal to an outsider.[3]

Jackson is dismissive of the 'Celtic Revival' of the end of the nineteenth century, as also of the the dim 'Celtic Twilight' (Yeats's term) of 'mournful, languishing, mysterious melancholy'. He concludes:

The Celtic literatures are about as little given to mysticism or sentimentality as it is possible to be; their most outstanding characteristic is rather their astonishing power of imagination.[4]

It is good to be called to order lest, in spite of periodic *caveats*, we conclude this brief study with a romanticism which sees only what it wants to see and hears only what it wants to hear. It is only fair, however, to remember that what Jackson calls 'mysticism' is probably not what I mean by that very overworked and imprecise term, but rather what I would describe as 'false mysticism'.

In terms of Christian mysticism – very much a 'down-to-earth' business – the Celtic writings are brim-full of it as we have seen, and not a hint of falsehood or of sentimentality anywhere, or indeed of romanticism. To get to heaven you have to keep your feet on the ground.

It is in fact the astonishing power of the Celtic imagination which is the key to this, for the imagination is that faculty within us which produces images. The power of the Celtic imagination is witness to the blessed vitality of its interior life and of the healthy and uninhibited vigour of its intuition. God 'speaks' through the intuitive faculty in the first instance, and the imagination clothes what is 'said' in appropriate images, both for the purpose of our own reception of the communication and also that it may be possible for us to communicate it to others.

At this point it will be helpful to introduce an important Christian insight, perhaps best articulated by Saint Gregory Palamas, a mystic of the Eastern Church. It concerns the vital distinction between the 'essence' of God and the 'energies' of God, these terms being employed – like any other theological terms – for want of better ones.

Briefly: God is unimaginable, unknowable by mankind or any other created being in His essence. Of that, nothing can be either said or known. But God is very much encountered and known in His energies. Everything we experience of God, everything revealed of God, everything in which God is 'known' (as opposed to 'known about') relates to His energies and not to the unknowable essence.

Thus the whole of Creation derives from God's energies, and in those terms is the transfigured image of its Creator. Thus the Blessed Trinity, that eternal love-affair which is God the Unity, is revealed to us through the divine energies. Of the divine essence we can only be silent.

There is an Indian story about the sage pointing to the moon with his finger. The idiot looks only at the finger! All the creeds, doctrines, dogmas and the rest, belonging to the Christian Church, are only pointing fingers; they can be no more, and it belongs to them to point faithfully and in truth. The very institution of the Church itself is but the sage pointing his finger. It remains depressingly true, however, that the idiot still looks only at the finger!

A thousand years before Saint Gregory Palamas, the Palamite insight was shared vividly by the Celt. It may be that our fascination with our aboriginal origins derives from an uneasy feeling that, like the idiot, we have become preoccupied with the pointing finger and have omitted to notice that all it can do is point.

In Celtic spirituality we see eyes looking beyond the pointing finger. They invite us to look with them.

And here we come to the correction of the very title of this book. It is not about Celtic Christianity at all because there is no such thing. It is not about the Celtic Church either, because there never was one, separate and definable in such terms. It is about *Celtic spirituality*, and there is indeed something vitally different and distinct about that.

THE NEED FOR CELTIC SPIRITUALITY TODAY

My walk this day with God,
My walk this day with Christ,
My walk this day with Spirit,
*   The Threefold all-kindly:*
*   Ho! ho! ho! the Threefold all-kindly.*

My shielding this day from ill,
My shielding this night from harm,
Ho! ho! both my soul and my body,
*   Be by Father, by Son, by Holy Spirit:*
*   By Father, by Son, by Holy Spirit.*

Be the Father shielding me,
Be the Son shielding me,
Be the Spirit shielding me,
*   As Three and as One:*
*   Ho! ho! ho! as Three and as One.*
                                        'Ceum na Corach'[5]

The Hebrew name Adam is derived from a similar word which means 'the dust of the earth'. Thus humanity is to be understood, in Biblical terms, as 'talking and thinking dust'. In a world of ever more advanced technology, of frenetic mobility and all the rest, it is very easy for present-day men, women and their children to become almost entirely divorced from their proper context which is 'the dust of the

*Ox of St. Luke with halo and cross. Gospel of
St. Matthew. Book of Kells.*

earth'. To become so split-off is to lose touch with reality. The Ash Wednesday reminder: 'Remember that you are dust, and to dust you shall return,' and its graveside fulfilment: 'Ashes to ashes, dust to dust,' are not at all in accord with the spirit of the present age!

Carmichael tells us:

> When the people of the isles come out in the morning, to their fishing, to their farming, or to any of their various occupations anywhere, they say a short prayer called *Ceum na Corach*, The Path of Right, The Just or True Way. If the people feel secure from being overseen or overheard they croon, or sing, or intone their morning prayer in a pleasing musical manner. If, however, any person, and especially if a stranger, is seen in the way, the people hum the prayer in an inaudible undertone peculiar to themselves, like the soft murmur of the ever-murmuring sea, or like the far-distant eerie sighing of the wind among the trees, or like the muffled cadence of far-away waters, rising and falling upon the fitful wind.[6]

The identification of mankind with Creation, and of Creation with mankind, is here both natural and complete. Mankind is God's priest to Creation, the ever-open door through which the divine love flows. Cut off from his context, man is robbed of his very meaning. It is small wonder that the urban sophisticate inhabits a world of diminishing reality – and insists that this cloud-cuckoo-land of fantasy is 'the real world'.

The spirituality of the Celt – 'Celtic Christianity', call it what you will – calls us back *to what we are*. It is a recall to reality. It is not 'religious'; life is so integrated, to such a degree are heaven and earth experienced in their unity, that there is nothing left to be 'religious' about. There is, after all, no 'religion' in heaven! The spirituality of the Celt is the living of life with the head in the heart.

There is a clear link between the spirituality of the Celtic Church and the Creation-centred spirituality movement associated with the writings of Matthew Fox and others. This movement seeks to restore equilibrium between the Biblical understanding of the Blessed Creation and what is seen as an unbalanced preoccupation with the Fall and subsequent Redemption. As we have seen, Celtic spirituality was fully formed and mature before the world-rejecting influences from the Mediterranean world impinged upon it.

Carmichael made the not very surprising discovery that the traditional spirituality he found in the Highlands and Islands owed nothing whatever to either the contemporary Roman Catholic Church or to the Presbyterian Kirk. It was a spirituality handed down from generation to generation, quite independent of both the post-Reformation Church traditions. He concluded, perhaps a trifle romantically, that the poems and the prayers originated in the monasteries of Iona and Derry. What is certain is that they stand closer to the source than either of the ecclesiastical traditions they complement.

They complement, and they also correct. The purpose, either of writing such a book as is here offered, or of reading it, must be the ensuing resolve to do something about it, for something urgently requires to be done. It is not possible to 'change the Church' (the perennial desire of the newly-ordained clergy), it is only possible to change oneself. If that is done faithfully, the rest will follow.

THE GREENNESS OF CELTIC SPIRITUALITY

Guard for me my feet upon the gentle earth of Wales.
Eleventh-Century Welsh[7]

To what was our anonymous eleventh-century Welsh-man referring? To his own safeguarding, or to his stewardship, his priesthood, to the gentle earth itself? Probably both, but he did not have to be told that it was 'the gentle earth' and that it must be treated not only with respect but also with love, for God loves it.

Celtic spirituality is 'green' through and through, and quite unselfconsciously. It approaches every-thing in personal terms, again unconsciously. It was never necessary to articulate the proposition that a personal Creator would be unlikely to create anything that was not – in some sense – a person. There are no 'things', for everything is a person. The insights of a Teilhard de Chardin, that consciousness is inherent in the hydrogen atom, is wholly consistent with the Celtic vision of things and, indeed, of the Celtic experience of things.

The hazards attending any expressions of original thought at the time of the Renaissance of learning led directly to the conscious separation of science from theology. This led inexorably to two morbid states of affairs; the first was the separation of science from its own 'soul', and the second was the divorce of religion from life. Such is our conditioning in this schizoid state of affairs that the total integration of Celtic spirituality will either challenge and convince – or seem quite extraordinary and rather quaint.

The rape of the gentle earth and the poisoning of the environment by the industrial man, and by the technological man who is succeeding him, might well have been impossible but for the two tragic splits in the human personality referred to above. Our growing awareness of responsibility for the world in which we live is born of fear lest we render it finally uninhabitable, and also from the realization that finite resources are in fact finite. Our emerging 'greenness' is thus a self-conscious affair. The spirituality of the Celt can help us to put our heads into our hearts. Only thus will 'concern for the environment' turn into the unself-conscious vision of Creation as the transfigured image of its Creator, and ourselves as 'talking and thinking dust' – and yet stewards and priests to the gentle earth and all its creatures.

Thankfully, the Celtic vision can see beyond industrial pollution to find God's glory in the midst of it, as Gwenallt Jones's poem 'Pigeons' testifies:

> They would circle about in the smoke-filled sky
> Giving colour to the twisted gloom;
> Lumps of beauty in the midst of the haze;
> The Holy Ghost's image above the Cwm.
>
> The Holy Ghost sanctifying the smoke,
> Turning worker to person of flesh and blood.
> The cash nexus transformed in the order of grace
> And the Unions part of the household of God.
>
> Gwenallt Jones, 'Pigeons'[8]

THE NEED FOR DOWN-TO-EARTH LOVE

> I see angels on clouds
> Coming with speech and friendship to us.
>
> Carmina Gadelica[9]

Intellectualism will never see angels on clouds, the rationalist mind is closed to the possibility – and is thus excluded from the experience.

Colmcille left Ireland under a cloud, following the battle of Cul-dreibne, there having been excommunication proceedings started against him, but for offences which Adomnan describes as 'venial and pardonable'. While this was in progress, Brendan, founder of the monastery at Birr, saw Colmcille approaching. At that moment Brendan's consciousness was altered and he later testified:

I saw a pillar, trailing fire and very bright, going before this man of God whom you despise, and holy angels accompanying him on his journey over the plain. I do not dare, therefore, to treat this man with scorn, who I see is predestined by God to lead the peoples to life.[10]

Brendan's testimony proved decisive, and the proceedings against Colmcille were dropped. Shortly afterwards, he set sail with his twelve companions for Iona.

I would feel happier about the health of my own contemporary Church of England if I thought that a similar testimony were to prove decisive at a Consistatory Court or at a meeting of General Synod. I do not rule it out, but the climate is inclined rather more towards academic, rationalistic scepticism.

> Come, Mary, and milk my cow,
> Come, Bride, and encompass her,
> Come, Columba the benign,
> And twine thine arms around my cow.
> Ho my heifer, ho my gentle heifer . . .
> My heifer dear, gentle and kind.
> For the sake of the High King, take to thy calf.
> Carmina Gadelica[11]

There is no separation in love between Mary the Mother of God, Saint Bride (including the pagan goddess she has assimilated), Colmcille/Columba, the heifer, the calf or yourself, gentle reader! Any separation exists only in a tragically separated mind. Or perhaps in a mind so conditioned by rationalism, or inhibited by mistaken post-Reformation confusion about 'invocation of saints', as to have been rendered virtually unreceptive to a whole dimension of normality.

The Celtic Christian tradition lacks the visual richness of the Eastern Orthodox, whose churches are filled with icons of the saints – but the underlying awareness is the same. The icons proclaim the ever-surrounding presence and fellowship of heaven, and the icons, in Orthodoxy, are seen as *sacramental presences* of those whom they represent. Thus St Seraphim of Sarov (*d*. 1833):

> . . . saw our Lord Jesus Christ in his aspect of Son of man, appearing in dazzling glory surrounded by the heavenly host, the seraphim and cherubim. He was walking through the air, coming from the west door towards the middle of the church . . . transfigured, he went into his icon by the Royal Door.[12]

The Celtic devotion to Mary, the Mother of God, is entirely 'down to earth' and unsentimental. There are none of the absurd possibilities, such as Anthony de Mello records, of the group of a thousand devotees of 'Our Lady of Guadaloupe' who went on a pilgrimage of reparation to Mexico City because the Bishop of the diocese had declared 'Our Lady of Lourdes' patroness of the diocese! In the minds of the devout, one 'our Lady' was apparently upstaging and in competition with another 'our Lady'! As he comments: 'That's the trouble with religion, if you 'don't watch out!' It is down-to-earth love, not religion, that calls:

> *Come, Mary, and milk my cow.*

It is down-to-earth love, not religion, that will experience the reality of her love, her fellowship, her reality.

CELTIC INTUITION AND THE 'SIGHT'

> *The man-child of longsided Ethne,*
> *As a sage he is a-blossoming.*
> *Colmcille, pure without blemish.*
> > *It is not oversoon to perceive him.*[13]

Adomnan, the biographer of Colmcille, records the foretelling of the saint's birth attributed to Mauchte of Louth, a fifth-century disciple of Saint Patrick. However this is to be understood, the phenomenon known as 'the sight' is far from rare in the Highlands and the Isles. It is not sought, however, and it is held in respect, even fear. Not every 'sight' is welcome.

My own grandfather, a splendid old Highlander who died when I was two years of age, took his first look at me and prophesied: 'The boy will be a writer!'

The intuitive sense, in all its manifestations, is never inhibited or denied in the context of Celtic spirituality. Its denial in Scots and Northern Irish Calvinism is wholly untypical of the Celtic tradition, and represents somewhat of an accident in religious history.

The rationalist cast of mind has difficulty with the Columban commonplace:

On a Tuesday, the saint spoke to the brothers as follows: 'Tomorrow, being Wednesday, we propose to fast. However, a troublesome guest will appear and our customary fast will be broken.'[14]

Colmcille's gift of the 'sight', usually about small matters but sometimes about greater, has been the subject of much rationalization among scholars. But I have encountered it frequently – sometimes startlingly – among such parishioners as I have cared for in thirty years. I have even had it myself, on occasion.

Our Lord, introduced to Nathaniel by his friend Philip, said: 'Here is an Israelite worthy of the name; there is nothing false in him.' Nathaniel asked him, 'How do you come to know me?' and Jesus replied, 'I saw you under the fig-tree before Philip spoke to you.'

Rationalistic 'explainings away' raise more questions than ever they answer.

A friend of mine, latterly a priest, was so accustomed to sometimes being in two places at once that he thought everyone did it – until he discovered differently! He came to understand the hazards that can attend such phenomena, and the extreme peril of their misuse. During his last years as a priest, however, he found the same faculty, on an altogether higher level, activated in him in the context of prayer on those rare occasions when it was appropriate to a priestly ministry. There was nothing odd about him, or about Colmcille, except perhaps that they were both Celts!

Celtic spirituality takes the total person in its stride and denies nothing, shies away from nothing, consecrates everything. It also 'remembers its manners' and keeps a respectful distance from those things that are not its concern – but without denying them.

O holy God of Truth,
O loving God of mercy,
Sign me from the spells,
Sign me from the charms . . .

Compassionate God of life,
Screen me from the bane of the fairy women . . .
                              Carmina Gadelica[15]

HAVE COMPASSION FOR THE 'SHADOW SIDE'

Bai yw melltithio bywyd.
(To curse life is to err)

                              Euros Bowen[16]

Saint Augustine of Hippo has, inescapably, emerged from these pages as the villain of the piece. But, reader, have compassion upon him! He shared with generations as late as that of my own parents (who died in the 1950s) a complete ignorance of the kind of psychological self-knowledge now available and commonplace among intelligent readers of magazine articles.

He was a child of his times and of his culture and, being the kind of man he was, the only way he could come to terms with severe sexual and personal problems was to rationalize them theologically into a spiritual pessimism which made some kind of sense to him – even if it was all wrong!

Had Saint Augustine been so fortunate as to encounter a C.G. Jung in his lifetime, the history of Western Christian spirituality might have been less fraught. It was Jung who commented that he had never encountered a sexual problem that was not also a religious problem, nor a religious problem that was not also a sexual problem. The matters we have been dealing with represent the shadow side – the tragic side – of an otherwise luminous personality. In other respects the Church's gratitude to Saint Augustine of Hippo remains undiminished.

Nor should we pass too ready judgements upon either John Calvin or Cornelius Otto Jansen, which latter devoured the darker writings of St Augustine thirty times before articulating his own gloom. They too were children of their times, and dark times they were, darker by far than our own.

The Christian Faith bids us to hate the sin but love the sinner. We can have nothing but compassion for those whose thinking was forced into distortion in a sincere search for truth in terrible times. But we are equally bound to recognize the distortion for what it is, and to act accordingly. But beware!

> Books burning in the fire.
> The horror of the burning is
> As ever, as ever, a sign.

> In the night, round about, there are bright eyes
> Full of the passion of destruction . . .
>
> Tomorrow,
> People in the fire.
>
> Gwyn Thomas[17]

As Laurens Van Der Post testifies of his own youth in South Africa:

> The vast complex of the consequence of a compulsive suppression of sex in the mind and customs of man was so great that one could easily see why, as Freud implied, it could appear as the villain in almost every piece of human folly and individual and cultural derangement. Even the Victorian dancing, just becoming fashionable in our late-Edwardian colonial day, was regarded as sinful.
>
> A young girl I knew, for instance, was badly beaten with a length of rope by her eldest brother because she had taken part in an impromptu dance in a house where she happened to be staying. Woman's place was so much confined to the home, kitchen and nurseries, that one of my own sisters had sermons preached against her in our local church because she had the presumption to become one of the first of her sex to go to a university and take a degree.[18]

We know better now. Celtic spirituality teaches us a better understanding of our own Christian Faith; it stands much closer to the source. All we have to do is allow ourselves to be taught by it.

TURAS – THE JOURNEY

The inspiration of the Wales that is to be
comes from the graves of the Wales that was.
Ben Bowen, translated by S. and C. Davies[19]

A Highland woman, Catherine Maclennan, told Alexander Carmichael how she and all the children were taught to start each day:

> My mother would be asking us to sing our morning song to God down in the back-house, as Mary's lark was singing it up in the clouds and as Christ's mavis [a throstle or song-thrush] was singing it yonder in the tree, giving glory to the God of the creatures for the repose of the night, for the light of the day, and for the joy of life. She would tell us that every creature on the earth here below and in the ocean beneath and in the air above was giving glory to the great God of the creatures and the worlds, of the virtues and the blessings, and would *we* be dumb![20]

A book, published in both Irish and English language editions in 1990, describes the Stations of *Turas Cholmcille*:

> Christian pilgrims visiting several holy places in Ireland perform set exercises and say prescribed prayers at one of a series of stations. The course they follow is called in Irish *an Turas*, literally 'the Journey'. The custom, particularly that of visiting holy wells, is widespread. The stations are marked by early Christian decorated cross-slabs or crosses at a number of important sites . . .
>
> At Glencholmcille the pilgrim doing *an Turas* circles the edge of the valley completing the set prayers and devotions at each station . . . Each station is normally circled three times sunwise (deiseal), keeping the right hand next to the station . . . The prayers said at each station are the *Credo*, and the *Pater* and *Ave*. The pilgrim, who is barefoot, travels a distance of about five kilometres, crossing the floor of the

valley twice and climbing a steep 100 metres to Colmcille's Well. The whole *Turas* takes three to four hours and is normally performed on St Colmcille's feast-day, the 9th of June.[21]

Prayer is an act of love. It is something *done* before ever it is something said. Earthly life is a journey, more truthfully, a pilgrimage to be discovered in the end as having been all of a piece. It is – or it is given to us in order to be – one great act of love, and is of course a mystery beyond our fathoming.

Creation is blessed and we partake of that blessing. Mankind is redeemed and made new, and all Creation is partaker of that making new. The Christian Faith, the Faith of the Celt, teaches us all over again our stewardship – our priesthood – of the good earth and of our brothers and sisters, its creatures. The Celtic Christian tradition can, if we will allow it to do so, rescue us from a vision grown too narrow, a God, interpreted in our own image, who is far too small and a cramped, bickering ecclesiasticism masquerading as the entire Kingdom of God. It can set our feet back firmly in the Way.

And now a blessing, dear reader, for your own *Turas*:

> *May God make safe to you each steep,*
> *May God make open to you each pass,*
> *May God make clear to you each road,*
> *And may He take you in the clasp*
> *of His own two hands.*
> Carmina Gadelica[22]

TEXTUAL REFERENCES

Chapter 1. The Relevance of our Celtic Roots

1. Jackson, K.H. (translator), *A Celtic Miscellany*, Penguin, 1971, p.86.
2. Van Der Post, L. *Jung and the Story of Our Time*, Penguin, 1978.
3. Campbell, J. *The Power of Myth*, Doubleday, 1988.
4. Jackson, p.74.
5. Scott, A.B. *The Pictish Nation: its People and its Church*, Foulis, 1918.
6. Delaney, F. *The Celts*, Grafton, 1989.
7. Scott.
8. Delaney, *The Celts*.
9. Meyer, K. (translator), *Selections from Ancient Irish Poetry*, Constable, 1959.
10. Gardner, W.H. and Mackenzie, N.H. (editors) *The Poems of Gerard Manley Hopkins*, Oxford University Press, 1967, p.66.
11. Jackson, p.86.
12. Yeats, W.B. *Selected Poems*, ed. A.N. Jeffares, Macmillan, 1963.
13. Jackson, p.300.
14. Van Der Post.
15. Maclean, G.R.D. (editor) *Praying with the Highland Christians*, Triangle Books/SPCK, 1961.
16. Jackson, p.284.

Chapter 2. Who Are These People?

1. Kinsella, T. (translator) *Tain Bo Cuailnge*, Oxford University Press, 1970.
2. Diodorus Siculus *History*, ed. C.H. Oldfather, London, 1933.
3. Delaney, *Legends of the Celts*, Grafton, 1991, p.15.
4. *ibid*, p.5.
5. *ibid*, p.135.
6. Kinsella, T. *New Oxford Book of Irish Verse*, Oxford University Press, 1968, p.3.

Chapter 3. The Faith Among the Britons

1. Evans, K.M. *A Book of Welsh Saints*, Church in Wales Publishing, 1967, p.31.
2. Sherley-Price, L. (translator) *Bede: History of the English Church and People*, Penguin, 1955, p.31.
3. *ibid*, p.185.

Chapter 4. Theological, Psychological – or Pathological?

1. Shirley-Price, p.76.
2. *ibid*, p.79.
3. Jackson, p.280.
4. Mascall, E.L. (translator) *Grace and Glory*, Faith Press, 1961, p.82.
5. *ibid*.
6. Jackson, p.109.

Chapter 5. The Conversion of Wales, Scotland and Ireland

1. O'Malley, B. (editor), S. and C. Davies (translators) *A Welsh Pilgrim's Manual*, Gomer, 1989, p.90.
2. Evans.

3. Jones, G. (editor) *The Oxford Book of Welsh Verse in English*, Oxford University Press, 1977, p.249.
4. Tennyson, A. Lord *Idylls of the King*, Airmont, 1969.
5. Jackson, p.72.
6. Scott.
7. *ibid*.
8. *ibid*.
9. *ibid*.
10. Mackie, J.D. *A History of Scotland*, Pelican, 1964.
11. Meyer.
12. Delaney, *The Celts*.
13. Marsden, J. *The Illustrated Columcille*, Macmillan, 1991, p.22.

Chapter 6. The Centuries of Sorrows

1. Jackson, p.263.
2. *ibid*, p.252.
3. Carmichael, A. (translator) *Carmina Gadelica*, Vol. III, Scottish Academic Press, 1928, p.339.
4. O'Malley, p.110.
5. Maclean, p.432.
6. O'Malley, p.110.
7. Carmichael, *Carmina Gadelica*, Vol. III, p.105.
8. *ibid*, Vol. III, p.307.

Chapter 7. Celtic? Catholic? Or Simply Orthodox?

1. O'Malley.
2. Jackson, p.206.
3. *ibid*, p.281.
4. Docherty, C. *Poustinia*, Collins, 1975.
5. *ibid*.
6. *ibid*.
7. Jackson, p.281.
8. Carmichael, *Carmina Gadelica*, Vol. I, p.293.
9. *ibid*, Vol. I, pp.183–5.
10. *ibid*, Vol. III, p. 169.

11. *ibid*, Vol. I, p.175.
12. Jackson, *A Celtic Miscellany*.

Chapter 8. Celtic Christianity – So What?

1. Carmichael, *Carmina Gadelica*, Vol. III, p.29.
2. Thomas, C. *Celtic Britain*, Thames & Hudson, 1986.
3. Jackson.
4. *ibid*.
5. Carmichael, *Carmina Gadelica*, Vol. III, p.49.
6. *ibid*.
7. O'Malley, p.34.
8. Clancey, J.P. (editor) *Twentieth-Century Welsh Poems*, Gomer, 1982, p.99.
9. Carmichael, *Carmina Gadelica*, Vol. I, p.13–19.
10. Zander, V. *St Seraphim of Sarov*, SPCK, 1975, p.9.
11. Carmichael, *Carmina Gadelica*, Vol. I, p.271.
12. Zander.
13. Marsden, p.42.
14. Mello, Anthony de *Awareness*, Fount, 1990, p.64.
15. Carmichael, *Carmina Gadelica*, Vol. III, p. 65–7.
16. O'Malley, p.92.
17. *ibid*, p.142.
18. Van Der Post.
19. O'Malley, p.84.
20. Carmichael, *Carmina Gadelica*.
21. Herity, M. *Gleanncholmcille*, Togra Ghleannocholmcille Teoranta, 1990.
22. Carmichael, *Carmina Gadelica*, Vol. III, p.202.

BIBLIOGRAPHY

Bede, *History of the English Church and People*, trans. L. Sherley-Price, Penguin, 1955.

Campbell, J. *The Power of Myth*, Doubleday, 1988.

Clancey, J.P. (ed.) *Twentieth-Century Welsh Poems*, Gomer, 1989.

Cross, F.L. *The Oxford Dictionary of the Christian Church*, Oxford University Press, 1957.

de Mello, A. *Awareness*, Fount, 1990.

de Waal, E. (ed.) *The Celtic Vision*, DLT, 1988.

Delaney, F. *The Celts*, Grafton, 1989.

— *Legends of the Celts*, Grafton, 1989.

Evans, K.M. *A Book of Welsh Saints*, Church in Wales Publishing, 1967.

Farmer, D. H. *The Oxford Dictionary of Saints*, Clarendon Press, 1978.

Foster, R.F. *Modern Ireland 1600–1972*, Penguin, 1989.

Fox, M. *Original Blessing*, Bear & Co., 1983.

Herm, G. *The Celts*, Weidenfeld, 1976.

Jackson, K.H. (trans.) *A Celtic Miscellany*, Penguin, 1971.

Jones, Gwyn (ed.) *The Oxford Book of Welsh Verse in English*, London, 1977.

Kinsella, T. (trans.) *The Oxford Book of Irish Verse*, Oxford University Press, 1986.

—*Tain Bo Cuailnge*, Oxford University Press, 1970.

Mac Eacharna, D. *The Lands of Lordship*, Argyll Reproductions, 1976.

Mackie, J. D. *A History of Scotland*, Pelican, 1964.

Maclean, G.R.D. *Praying with Highland Christians*, Triangle/ SPCK, 1988.

Marsden, J. *The Illustrated Colmcille*, Macmillan, 1991.

Mascall, E. L. *Grace and Glory*, Faith Press, 1961.

Matthew, Sir T. (trans.) *St Augustine: Confessions*, Fontana, 1957.

Matthews, C. *The Elements of the Celtic Tradition*, Element Books, 1989.

Meyer, K. (ed.) *Selections from Ancient Irish Poetry*, Constable, 1959.

O'Donnell, M. (ed.) *Betha Colaim Chille*, A. O'Kellehar & G. Schoepperle, 1918.

O'Malley, B. (ed.) *A Welsh Pilgrim's Manual*, Gomer, 1989.

Scott, A. B. *The Pictish Nation: its People and its Church*, Foulis, 1918.

Thomas, C. *Celtic Britain*, Thames & Hudson, 1986.

Tunney, J. *St Colmcille and the Columban Heritage*, St Colmcille Heritage Trust, 1987.

Van Der Post, L. *Jung and the Story of Our Time*, Penguin, 1978.

Waddell, H. (trans.) *Medieval Latin Lyrics*, Penguin, 1952.

Ware, T. *The Orthodox Church*, Penguin, 1963.

Wood, M. *Domesday: A Search for the Roots of England*, BBC Publications, 1986.

Zander, *St Seraphim of Sarov*, SPCK, 1975.

INDEX